THE
WAYS
AND
POWER
OF
LOVE

C. KAY ALLEN

To Doris, my wife and companion of
forty-four years, and to my family.

ABOUT THE AUTHOR

Widely recognized educator, businessman, community leader, lecturer, and author, C. Kay Allen holds an M.S. degree in Educational Psychology. As a lecturer in the field of human relations, he has associated with three Colorado universities and Brigham Young University, where he was honored as Outstanding Teacher in 1977. He has actively contributed to the field of mental health by serving as chairman of the Utah State Board of Mental Health, as president of the Colorado Mental Health Association, and as a member of the Research and Prevention Committees of the National Association of Mental Health.

Allen has worked in different areas of public service and business. His public service career spans state legislatures and community education. He was the speaker of the Utah House of Representatives from 1965 to 1967 and the chairman of three separate organizations: Utah's Coordinating Council of Health and Welfare Services, the State Legislative Council, and the Governor's Housing Committee. In 1967 he was instrumental in organizing a rural school construction program sponsored by Partners of the Alliance, under which Utah school children raised all of the required funding that paid for the construction of twenty-six schools by native Bolivians in rural Bolivian locations. Since 1975, he has been a contributing member of the Denver Interfaith Council in the areas of radio and television programming and public workshops. In the area of business, Allen has worked in banking and commercial real estate development and investment since 1958. He established several financial institutions in Colorado and served as director for several commercial banks and two insurance companies.

Using his expertise in business and leadership and his experience in the field of human relations, he successfully founded and directed two institutes: the Human Values Institute, an organization that disseminates ideas and techniques of team development and communication, and that helps organizations function more effectively, and the Human Development Institute, a counseling and teaching center that helps individuals accept personal responsibility for their attitudes, performance, quality of life, and relationships. He continues his efforts to strengthen individuals by conducting workshops and seminars, providing personal counseling, and giving lectures. In addition, he is the author of *Journey from Fear to Love* and *Personal Empowerment,* two books that deal with issues related to his experience with people.

Father of four and grandfather of fifteen, C. Kay Allen has held many educational and religious positions. While serving as an instructor, he taught for nineteen years in a variety of programs including the Know Your Religion series, BYU Education Week, and On-Campus Education Week. While he was a member of the Writing Committee of the LDS church, he developed and wrote several church manuals. He has also been a bishop, a high councilor, and a member of the Sunday School General Board of that church. Currently, he teaches a doctrinal Sunday School class. He lives in Denver, Colorado.

CONTENTS

PREFACE

This book has been about ten years in the making and is the crowning point of a larger thirty-year effort. It is based on an expansive idea which has resulted in four books, eight workbooks, a number of audio tapes, and countless working papers.

For me and my family, two significant, life-shaping difficulties also occurred during this same period of time: First, in the declining Denver real estate market that has not yet recovered, we lost our material possessions, leaving us with perhaps two or three percent of what we once owned. Second, I lost my health and physical strength as I suffered nine heart attacks and probably two more that were not recorded in hospital reports. Because of the massive deterioration that destroyed sixty percent of my heart, I required two quadruple heart bypass operations and I still suffer rather severe daily bouts with angina pectoris.

While I am not sure I should reveal such personal aspects of my life, I feel it is significant that this book was born and written in my family's "fiery furnace." Throughout these years, I have learned that I could always count on my family to be gently accepting and encouraging when the hurt was deep and the failures seemed constant. They did not weaken me with pity or sympathy. Instead, they helped me face each day with courage and determination.

When we had conflicts or were irritable with one another, we admitted our differences quickly and looked beyond them because we knew that our relationships were more important than our problems. We were acutely aware of what created trust or weakened it, and we were deeply committed to working to develop win-win situations in our relationships with one another. During the times when our problems seemed too overwhelming to handle, we learned to surrender to the grace of God by seeking his comfort and relying on his strength in our lives.

I cite these facts in order to further acknowledge my family's contributions to this labor of love recorded in book form. I want to say a few things to them personally. First to Doris, my wife: Through these difficult years, you have borne all of these burdens with me, demonstrating constant acceptance and strength. Often when my hand was weak and unsteady, yours was strong. Rather than give in to your fears that I would have another heart attack, you decided to accept and enjoy what each day had to offer and to live each day in the moment. During all this, you had great faith and abiding love. No words can adequately express how grateful I am to you

My thanks to Connie and Brian for your incredible faith and your knowledge of eternal realities beyond this mortal existence. I thank you for the example you gave us when you adopted two Peruvian girls, Maria and Jessica, whom you raised in love with your own children, Spenser and Kelly. I thank you for your kind, generous hearts and for giving, not because of duty, but because you love to give. I thank you for keeping in touch with me and my family even though you lived out of state. I thank you for not allowing financial success to corrupt your humility and desire to share with others.

I express my gratitude to Roger and Judy and your children, Melinda, Jonathan, and Cheryl-Lynn, for a safe place to be and say anything, where I know that whatever I say will not be judged and that everything said will be given the honor of a confidence. I thank you for establishing a good home where children are valued, where learning is revered, and where life is viewed as an exciting challenge and a wonderful opportunity for growth. I thank Roger for your tireless assistance as I developed the Love/Trust Model and for developing classes so full of love, compassion, and toughness that they transform those who attend.

My love and appreciation goes to Rolayne and Kent and your children, Dave, Brian, Nathan, and Lindsay, for always being there, for being sensitive and aware of our needs, and helping us when we needed help but did not ask for it. I thank you for allowing me the privilege of watching your children grow up, thus giving my sometimes tired, old blood some exciting new young tonic.

I express my admiration especially to Rolayne for creating of your home a place of safety and growth for countless young girls who have lost their way, modeling for them mature behavior and life-affirming principles, and for teaching your children by love and example how to make a family work.

Thanks to Paul and Jackie, and your children, Amber, Doug, Jason, and Tim, for also creating a good home where children can flourish and grow, and for exemplifying a purity and an innocence that almost surpass my understanding—it is simply what you are; for your optimism and faith that come from within both of you and for your service which you give, never seeking to count the cost and without expecting public recognition or reward. I thank Paul for your endless help as our financial world crumbled beneath my feet, for holding on to the last, for running interference and blocking what problems you could, for assembling data, files, and reports, and for performing a thousand services I so desperately needed—I can never thank you enough.

The family is an incomparable workshop for learning and teaching Christlike love and attributes. I express thanksgiving for the continuing health of our fifteen grandchildren and for the give-and-take that has brought all of us together in a home that has been a center of love and learning where we could deal with life on the terms given us. To my family members I offer my deepest appreciation for your unflagging support, for your commitment to the highest Christian ideals, and for what you have taught me about the ways and power of love. To you, my beloved family, I dedicate this book.

ACKNOWLEDGMENTS

I acknowledge first my dear friend, Randy Morrison, who has been a companion and confidant for many years. He has taught me that the writer's greatest power is in simplicity, not complexity. He also assisted me in drafting some chapters, seeking both to simplify and strengthen this work. Randy's wonderful peak experience, which lasted many weeks, was an inspiration to me at that time and has continued through many years. He has been my strongest critic and support, and I owe much of my discipline to him.

Second, I acknowledge Rolayne Allen Sellers, my daughter, for endless writing and rewriting of the manuscript and for her countless suggestions, that increased the clarity of this book. She has given me the rare gift of being a safe place and fully accepting me. I thank her for always being there for me.

My special appreciation to my editor at Covenant, Darla Hanks Isackson, who knows and values not only this book and the work on which it is based, but also the life-transforming power of the Human Development Institute classes. She knows that the principles, which are taught both in my book and these classes, give people a new way to see, a more adequate way to make decisions, and a more whole way to live and to love. Her understanding translated into a power to clarify and tighten the text and make this book say what I really meant. I also appreciate the valuable editing help received from Valerie Holladay and Holly Smith.

I acknowledge Lea Diane Engebretsen for her research and editing help. After I decided to deepen the spiritual power and orientation of this book, she wrote and rewrote portions of it with that orientation, thus strengthening its focus and Christ-centeredness. Thanks, also, for her wonderful poem.

Joy Young deserves acknowledgment for long discussions and editorial help with the last two ways of love and for the weeks she spent teaching me about what becoming a writer means. To my friend and fellow traveler on the road to understanding—thanks.

PART 1:
LAYING THE FOUNDATION

INTRODUCTION:
THE GROWTH PROCESS

A SEED THAT GOES INTO THE WARM, MOIST EARTH IS SHRIVELED, tiny, and dry. But the gardener is unconcerned about this, for he has seen what time and care will do for this packet of possibilities. He covers the seed with soil, gives the spot a good drenching, and goes away content to let the miracle of growth take place in darkness, hidden from the view of the world.

In time the wetness and the warmth coax open the shell of the seed and awaken the life sleeping within. A single, brave root burrows determinedly and an eager shoot breaks the surface, carrying on its shoulders the old shell. This protective skin, once crucial to survival, will soon be thrown off and forgotten, its mission fulfilled. The gardener is glad when he sees the green sprig, but he is not surprised. He knows that the force of life is the urge to grow just waiting for the chance.

The gardener provides the plant with an ideal beginning, but that is not enough. Throughout the season he must continue to make sure the plant gets enough water and is protected from temperature extremes, weeds, pests, and diseases. When he does these things, the plan of life encoded in the seed will quietly perform the thousand miracles of growth and development. Sunlight and carbon dioxide will be turned into energy for growth.

New cells will be created from the division of old ones, and some of the resulting cells will become different from what their parent cells were. Each cell will become specialized to respond to the needs of the maturing plant—becoming leaves to collect light, roots to support and absorb nutrients, stems and branches to extend, and buds and flowers to attract bees—all contributing to the final result: new seeds to start the cycle over again. This complete process happens without any effort at all by the gardener. The miraculous part is automatic!

These miracles of growth happen a million times a minute all over the world, and we are so confident of them we hardly ever notice. However, we need to develop the same sort of assurance toward our own growth process. Most of us are generally confident that our bodies will develop normally. However, we often feel exasperated concerning the nonphysical areas of growth (that is, the social, emotional, psychological, and spiritual aspects of our growth). This is not because our growth has no plan, but because we are not aware of it or do not know how to recognize and use it.

There is a plan—a mainstream path of growth and development for the human mind, heart, and soul, as well as for the body. We are creatures of nature, a manifest system of order and law. From the development of suns out of cosmic dust and the creation of grand canyons out of earthly dust to the creation of humans themselves, all things respond to law.

Some may protest that suns and canyons follow these patterns of growth because they are not thinking beings as we are. While this is true, our thoughts and choices can only be manifested through the physical world we live in, so our mental development must also follow a systematic plan of order.

We Must Learn to Be Our Own Gardeners

Here is the real difference between ourselves and the other elements of the physical world: although we too can depend on the impetus of life to accomplish most of the miracles, we must learn to be our own gardeners. We must learn to identify and remove the weeds, pests, and diseases that inhibit our growth. We must also learn to nurture our own development.

This means, primarily, learning how choices affect our growth. We must then learn to implement this understanding to develop the strength to make the choices which, in the long run, will contribute most to our progress toward self-actualization. This is a process I call "valuing" or the "Human Valuing System." To understand this valuing process, we need first to understand the different levels at which we live.

Three Levels of Living

Through our thoughts, attitudes, and habits, we choose the world in which we live, for we see primarily what we expect to see. For simplicity of understanding, the levels of living are divided into three stages: fear/anxiety, duty/justice, and love/trust.

The lowest level of living—so called because it is furthest from the fullest flowering of "human beingness"—is fear/anxiety. On this level, all of life is seen as a battle. It is underscored by its ubiquitous anxiety, for even the victor fears that some new warrior will rise up and take it all away from him. Personal worth for fear/anxiety people springs from "having"; that is, their mind-set sees everything, including other people, as objects to be possessed or controlled by whatever means necessary—be it force, restriction, or manipulation. Since all such possession is transitory, self-esteem at this level is low, tentative, and nervous.

In the fear/anxiety world, success is defined as survival, and most behavior springs from avoidance impulses; that is, we do only what we are afraid not to do and we avoid whatever causes us to respond with fear. Unhappy and unnatural as this state of living is, it seems to be a stage of development through which we all pass—or at least one which we all experience now and then. This world sends us endless fear/anxiety signals, and we must decide what to do with them.

The second level, duty/justice, is a much better world. Here we are not motivated by the law of the jungle, but by ideals of justice and honor that tell us what we "ought" to do. Decency and reliability replace the chaos and insecurity of fearful living so we can live with order and confidence. Such living brings discipline to our world and our relationships and helps us know what we can count on.

But dutiful living can bring an overemphasis on the letter of the law, formal systems, and scorekeeping. And if order becomes our supreme goal, our lives can become stultifying and boring. After a while, we ask, "Is this all there is?"

The answer is this: there *is* much more, and it is experienced in the love/trust world. This is the realm of high self-esteem, joy in daily living, and unconditional acceptance. Rather than avoiding punishment, as the fearful do, or seeking reward, as the dutiful do, trusters act because they receive inherent pleasure, satisfaction, and joy. Their open, willing, nonpossessive approach to life is called "being" by the philosophers. It is the attitudinal state achieved by the wisdom masters of all major religions. Living on this level results in the natural freedom of being fully human.

The Human Valuing System I mentioned earlier is fundamentally a set of concepts and skills designed to help people make the transition from fearful to dutiful to joyful living and from *having* to *doing* to *being*. I call the model for this system the love/trust model. This book deals both with our ability to grow into being and with the normal developmental stages of the love/trust life. The love/trust life does not deal with skills specifically; that sort of deliberateness is part of the growth into duty. Rather, it deals more with insights and attitudes in a descriptive way. Living the love/trust life is a highly individual matter, and we each work toward self-actualization in our own way.

Cycles of Learning and Growth

The main pathway of human growth goes from fear/anxiety to duty/justice to love/trust. Important lessons are to be learned at each step along the way. Growth is usually cyclical, beginning with a key insight and followed by an attempt to live in accordance with that insight. First tries are often clumsy but, with practice, we finally reach the heights that we initially saw as a glimmering light in the distance. From there, a new insight leads us onward again.

These moments of insight can be life-changing. To a person who has been stuck on the fear/anxiety level, a flash of "pre-being" may come as an abrupt insight triggered by some little comment at just the key moment. Such an insight might well include this realization: "I'm tired of living an angry, self-defeating life. I'm going to find a way out." If the person knows how to apply the insight, this may spark a major new personal growth spurt. If not, the struggler may get frustrated in his misdirected efforts and end up even more cynical than before.

For example, Bill may realize that it is better to be trusting than to be suspicious. But without learning to develop trust in worthy individuals, his efforts may result in his becoming victimized. We all know the old adage that a fool and his money are soon parted.

There are two stages to each cycle of learning. In the functional stage, we gain a vision of what we want to do. For instance, Bill needs to gain a vision of what it is to become more trusting. In the second, or structural, stage we learn how to implement the vision in our lives—in this example, to *develop* trust. Some of us, typically dreamers, artists, and other right-brained individuals, prefer to learn functionally, by getting the vision and then proceeding intuitively. Others—rationalists, analysts, scientists, and other left-brained individuals—emphasize structure and method. Though each group often disdains the approach of the other as either impractical or mechanical, the truth is that both methods are necessary. Great artists are scientists of their craft first, and great scientists use the artist's insight to lead them in their process of inquiry. To be fully human we must use both sides of the brain.

Cycles of Strengthening Behavior

In the process of becoming our own gardener, we need to learn to identify the weeds and pests that inhibit our growth and throw us off the mainstream of growth into unproductive tangents. Patterns of repetitive failure are collectively referred to as the cycle of failure or, in other words, weakening behavior. The major causes of learned failure are believing in false or weakening ideas, holding harmful assumptions, imitating poor role models, being ignorant of what constitutes human success, experiencing failure conditioning, and being unable to bridge the gap between the ideal and the real.

The antidote to this cycle of failure is the cycle of strengthening behavior, which consists of six concepts and their accompanying skills. These concepts are—

1. Awareness (knowing where you are)
2. Trust-building skills (creating safe and trusting conditions)
3. Breaking the cycle of hostility
4. Harnessing harmful behavior
5. Achieving the bedrock of trust
6. Learning the problem-solving skill of commitment

Before we are ready to begin learning and living the love/trust life, we must first master some basic lessons at the duty/justice stage—developing self-control and deep-level integrity in order to be congruent and real, eliminating the cop-out of blaming, and learning to work from our personal strengths. As we move into the love/trust

life, we will learn other important lessons, including handling interpersonal conflict productively, becoming truly accepting of ourselves
and others, becoming committed to win-win solutions and equal
relationships, and being teachable and open to new ideas. We will
also gain an understanding of the attitude sequence (having, doing,
being) and, perhaps paramount, we will realize that a better life is
possible.

What Is the Love/Trust Life?

Living the love/trust life means being drawn to other people in a
positive way and drawing them to you without strain or tension. It
means knowing that people always count more than things and
that you are valued even when you behave badly. At the love/trust
level people are not seen as enemies to be defeated or repelled, but
as fellow human beings who are attractive in their own right.
Living the love/trust life means being in tune with our best and
highest spiritual promptings.

The Power of Love

Love is rare in this world permeated by fear and hostility. Most of
us get only infrequent samples of love. But those sparse savorings
leave powerful memories, for they place all else in a new context of
what is possible. To feel the quiet power of love is to know beyond
knowledge that life is good and that the world is friendly. Despite
our limited experience with love, we have tasted enough to know
that we want more.

Love is the cohesive force. It draws us into greater union with
ourselves, brings us into harmony with others, and opens up the
world—indeed, the whole universe—as a place of peace and fundamental beneficence. When our hearts are in the territory of love
and trust, then the deepest and warmest waters of life flow most
freely: the waters of openness, caring, and sharing. The love/trust
life is infinitely and inherently worthwhile. This is because we are
rewarded *by* our virtue, not *for* our virtue. We are harmed *by* our
mistakes not *for* our mistakes.

Love transforms. Its power puts us right with the world and we
can then see that the world has always been right with us. No other

force on earth has the power of unfeigned and unrestrained love. No fiery anger can long continue to blaze in the calm face of complete acceptance. No diseased mind can long fail to respond to the healthy, magnetic glow of this loving aura. The defeated spirit leaving this life is still hungry for love and remains capable of complete renewal by this healing force. The touch of love restores life.

While there is darkness as well as light in the human mind, the light, the innate longing to be loving, is more fundamentally embedded than is the gloomiest discouragement. The design of nature is that hope may be dim for awhile, but the seed will not be lost. The taproot will grow again long after the trunk at the surface has disappeared. The urge to love is but the final manifestation of the first need: survival. In the perspective of eternity, we must love or die.

Self-Actualization and the Love/Trust Life

Self-actualization is best defined as the achievement of the love/trust life: we become aware of our own capacity to be loving. We understand love and how to use it because we are part of its abundant flow and because we sense how love is both a generous gift from a higher source and a gentle geyser from within ourselves. We let love live free in our hearts. All these things are part of the process of growing into the love/trust life. Although self-actualization is a universal goal, it is individual and unique in its expression and accomplishment.

Paradoxical as it may seem, individuality actually increases as we gain greater harmony with life. Consciousness of self is clearest when we see ourselves in the context of all of God's creations. Self-control is highest when we are most accepting of others. And, as we move through the normal stages of development in accordance with the plan of nature (called actualization in psychological circles), we move closer to the loving life, which can only be expressed in our own unique ways.

The Ways of Love

I call the five principal areas of expansion into the love/trust life the "ways of love." Like the laws governing the physical world, they are descriptions of how I interpret the Creator's design. In this case, we observe cause-and-effect relationships beyond the merely physical realm. The ways of love function sequentially and cumulatively in the order they appear in this book:

1. Acceptance and Awareness
2. Selection and Order
3. Internalization and Confirmation
4. Shared Meaning through Gift-giving
5. Oneness and Harmony

Usually, we will not move up to the next stage until we have mastered the previous stage. When one stage is internalized, then the following stage (based on the insights gained by experience) emerges out of it. This whole spiraling process is a gradual opening to the forces of growth, much as the plant grows from the single seed. Best of all, as we become our own gardeners, after we have mastered keeping the bugs and weeds out, we can relax, let go, and marvel in wonder as the miracle of growth occurs automatically!

CAN WE MAKE THE
IDEAL, REAL?

J OE BROWN SAT IN A SUNDAY SCHOOL CLASS AND HEARD, FOR THE
hundredth time, a well-presented lesson about leading with love
in the home and respecting his wife. It was the kind of lesson
and discussion he had heard and participated in for years. His teacher
had the class read in Ephesians, "Husbands, love your wives." For
the hundredth time, Joe was certain he was hearing a true principle.
He was also just as certain that no sooner would he and his wife
arrive home than they would become locked in a battle or psychological tug-of-war, casting blame on the other and trying to prove their
superiority. And then one of them would withdraw, sulk, or try to
punish the other in subtle or overt ways. In the end, each would be
left feeling more defeated after their argument than before.

Joe was mature enough to know that when he became argumentative and defensive, his wife responded defensively, a way of
responding that only made matters worse, further deteriorating the
situation. He was also aware that he frequently blamed his wife and
children for his own frustrations, although in his heart he knew that
blaming was hurtful and that whenever he proved he was "right," it
meant someone else was "wrong." This blaming hindered their
communication and built up barriers they could not tear down.

As he looked around the classroom, Joe wrestled with the thought
that something must be wrong with him. He didn't know how to
apply the ideal concepts he heard in church to his daily family life
nor could he translate those words and ideas into realistic behavior.
He felt he must have missed something that other men and their
families seemed to have grasped.

In quiet moments, when he thoughtfully and honestly considered
his life, Joe realized that although he was conducting his life and

affairs within the parameters of fairness, decency, duty, and honesty, something significant was missing from his life.

Joe's wife, Carol, shared a similar emptiness and dissatisfaction. She had observed other families who seemed content and satisfied, but beneath her positive efforts and outward appearance she felt an underlying sense of frustration and sadness. She longed for a deeper intimacy and soul-to-soul communication with her husband. During the times when she and Joe were able to communicate without hostility, they asked each other why they could not seem to pull together the realities of their life with the high ideals and concepts taught in the scriptures. Carol knew she genuinely loved Joe, but she nevertheless felt a distance and estrangement between them. She wanted and needed to feel that she was truly valuable in his life.

Joe sincerely loved Carol and was committed to her and to bringing about the well-being and happiness of their family. He was also confident in her loyalty and their mutual desire to live righteously. And yet their relationship was, at best, only partly successful.

Seeing Our World in a New Way

Like Joe and Carol, we may find ourselves having similar feelings. We may resort to seeing others or circumstances as the enemy and possibly blame our church for being entirely unrealistic in its high expectations of us. These tendencies are, however, self-defeating. Many of us, like Joe and Carol Brown, need to see our world in a new way.

This book deals with the power of love and how it can function in our lives; how we can understand and make the ideal and the real world come closer together in our lives and relationships; how we can give power to our commitments; how we can think in better, more productive ways about our relationships with our wives or husbands, children, coworkers, and associates; and how we can think in new ways about God and our relationship with him.

Since our level of self-esteem propels us into cycles of behavior that serve to either weaken or strengthen us, the most important judgments we make in this life are the ones we make about ourselves. Such internal judgments, sometimes conscious (though often not), become the basis of our self-esteem—how we feel about and value ourselves and what conclusions we have made about ourselves from data we have gathered since birth. The level of our self-esteem literally determines the way we see the world.

One thing I am deeply certain of is that God did not mean for us to fail. When the Savior walked among men, he assured us, "I am come that [all] might have life, and that they might have it more abundantly." (John 10:10.)

I am convinced that the Lord did indeed intend for us to live the abundant life and to find joy therein. For many years, I have sought after and pondered many of the commentaries, references, definitions, and words of the world's poets, philosophers, psychologists, social scientists, and prophets regarding "love." Through my fieldwork in counseling and psychology, my observation of people, my church experience, and my years of study on this subject, I have come to certain conclusions. One is that love operates according to eternal laws and manifests itself at various levels that are consistent with the order of the universe and other eternal immutable laws.

Eternal Laws in Operation Now

As I searched the scriptures and studied, I gained a conviction that telestial, terrestrial, and celestial laws are in operation *now*. In the New Testament the Apostle Paul says, "There are also celestial bodies, and bodies terrestrial: but the glory of the celestial is one, and the glory of the terrestrial is another. There is one glory of the sun, and another glory of the moon, and another glory of the stars: for one star differeth from another star in glory." (1 Corinthians 15:40-41.) Was Paul symbolically referring to persons, or to differing bodies in the celestial universe? His message was consistently to and about people, and it is likely that he was symbolically referencing the ways various individuals live their lives at different levels of being.

Whatever Paul was referring to, it is obvious that people do live at different levels of maturity, understanding, and being. As is briefly mentioned in the Introduction, we would be blind to the human condition if we did not recognize that these different levels exist. It is only when we understand the results or consequences produced by such varying life-styles that we are able to grow toward that which is more fulfilling.

Because of the passage in 1 Corinthians where Paul discusses the three levels, I began to ask, What are *telestial, terrestrial,* and *celestial* people really like in their families, business relationships, and personal lives? As I continued to explore these questions, I formulated a definition for three representative life-styles that are found on a continuum. The person at the telestial, or lowest, level of self-esteem operates at what I call the fear/anxiety level. People at this level are characterized by failure-producing behavior and deadening emotions. The person whose major mode of behavior originates at this level views other people with some degree of contempt, hostility, and fear. He has little respect for himself or others and, when confronted, will fight, ignore, or run from conflict. He has diminished awareness and capacity for growth and little self-control. He succeeds only in generating further conflict and alienation in his relationships.

A person at the terrestrial, or intermediate, level of self-esteem, operates at the duty/justice level—a level typified by actions and feelings that are based on fairness and regulated by duty and honor. This person is steady, dependable, and honest, and tries to obtain and accomplish all the normally accepted goals. He is motivated by what he thinks he "ought" to do, is capable of reasonable self-control, and may be interested in searching for help, harnessing harmful behaviors, and strengthening his commitments.

The individual with high self-esteem, who operates at a love/trust (or celestial) level, begins to experience his limitless capacity for forming open, satisfying relationships with others. He participates fully and productively in his work and possesses a self-confidence that comes from a deep sense of his own intrinsic worth. He exhibits quiet, deep self-control, and the ability to govern his life at high levels of meaning. He desires to create and build safe and trusting conditions, and harmony and acceptance in his relationships; he is motivated by feelings of genuine love and caring.

Our Levels of Existence

The resulting theoretical model of human behavior that I have developed centers around the concept that people live at these various levels of being. Motives, awareness, concepts, and skills are different on each level. Self-interest is always present but as we progress from one level to another, changes in our nature occur that alter our thinking and behavior.

This model, which has evolved over a period of years and has been field tested with thousands of people, is unique in its approach to teaching skills together with concepts—a process that enables people to empower themselves and change their lives.

These degrees of existence do not merely describe heaven, they are very apt descriptions of the vastly different kinds of lives I see people living every day. This book explores the conditions of these types of existence right now, in this life. Our behavior and what we actually do in our homes and personal lives is greatly affected by the degree of glory that we exemplify in our lives. Is there a telestial way of behaving? Is there a terrestrial way of behaving? And also a celestial way to act *now*, in this life? I believe there is.

As I sought further enlightenment in the scriptural record of how God's covenant people have lived and acted historically, I was reminded that when the children of Israel were delivered from Egyptian bondage into the wilderness, they wandered in fear and anxiety. They were literally like children in that they needed to be told exactly what to do; they needed to be controlled externally. Their prophet leader, Moses, patiently introduced them to the laws of fairness and justice in the great Ten Commandments, upon which all the laws of our American jurisprudence system are based. He sought to build controls into his people by teaching them to rise above fear/anxiety to operate at the duty/justice level. This level is based on laws designed to make people responsible for their actions.

The Celestial Law of Love

A thousand years after Moses lived, our Savior was born. He was a man of gentle strength who was a perfect example to a people entrenched in the letter of the law. He brought the new and higher law—the "good news"—the gospel, which framed the celestial law of love. This was not a new version of the law of duty and justice; rather, it was the law of charity, of which the Apostle Paul says, "And now abideth faith, hope, charity, these three; but the greatest of these is charity." (1 Corinthians 13:13.)

Loving Our Neighbors

The law of love, as Christ taught, is designed to make us responsible even for our thoughts; the law of love can ultimately set us free. He did away with the Mosaic law and brought the fullness and fulfillment of the law as John declares: "For the law was given by Moses, but grace and truth came by Jesus Christ." (John 1:17.) The

Apostle Paul also attests: "For all the law is fulfilled in one word, even in this; Thou shalt love thy neighbor as thyself." (Galatians 5:14.)

In contemplating our accountability under the higher law of the gospel, I am convinced that the great day of judgment is *not* the most important day in our lives. The most important day we will ever live is *today*. The decisions we make today and every day determine our level of existence. We are choosing our eternity now by the choices we make in regard to God's laws. God has never given us a commandment that was not intended for our long-term strengthening, character development, and progression toward perfection.

The scriptures are replete with the phrase that "every knee shall bow and every tongue confess that Jesus is the Christ." Implied in that truth is the fact that one day everyone will see sin for what it truly is—a destroyer, a wrecking bar, a producer of every possible form of unhealthiness and unhappiness. Further, when we acknowledge that sin is harmful, we will understand, believe, and seek after the abundant life that contains the joy and glory Christ has said is available and waiting for us.

The Apostle Paul declares, "Eye hath not seen nor ear heard, the things which God hath prepared for them that love him." (1 Corinthians 2:9.)

Loving God and Becoming Like Him

A celestial person, then, has begun the process of becoming more like God, so he is developing Godlike attributes. The scriptures tell us that our Father's most important attribute is love: God has so internalized love that *he is love*. (See 1 John 4:7-8.) When we ask what is the greatest of all commandments, we are assured that love is the highest and most noble quality we can develop as human beings. Our capacity to develop an increased amount of love is evidence of our potential divinity. When the Savior of the world said, "Love one another; as I have loved you" (John 13:34), he established the pattern and set up the equation. When one of the pharisees asked Christ which was the greatest commandment in the law, he said:

> Thou shall love the Lord thy God with all thy heart, and with all thy soul, and with all thy mind. This is the first and great commandment. And the second is like unto it, Thou shalt love thy neighbor as thyself. (Matthew 22:37-39.)

Loving Ourselves

Christ directed first that we love God with all our heart, might, mind, and strength—in other words, with total commitment. The second commandment is "like unto it"—that we love our neighbors as ourselves. Our ability to implement and live the two greatest commandments depends on our ability to truly *love ourselves.*

Selfish people do not love themselves too much, but rather too little. Since they don't feel right or good about themselves, they search for ways to make themselves look better than others or prove that they are superior to others. Charitable self-love is not selfishness. Loving and trusting ourselves fills us with the confidence we need to extend love and trust to others. When we are able to accept and cherish the person we know best, ourselves as individuals, we are then able to genuinely care for others.

Avoiding the Illusions of Love

Our problem with love is that we get trapped in the counterfeits and illusions of love. (I explain these in the next chapter.) These illusions may persuade us to think that we are loving someone or being loved, when we are only temporarily enabling another to feel better, or when another is, in fact, merely employing some artificial means to placate our deepest needs for love and approval.

Once we determine that something important is missing, we can learn to empower key moments of choice in our lives to enable us to live more positively and more abundantly. Key moments of choice are crucial steps in our eternal progression. Joshua showed his conviction in a key moment outside the walls of Jericho over a thousand years ago when he said, "Choose ye this day whom ye will serve . . . but as for me and my house, we will serve the Lord." (Joshua 24:15.)

One of the best ways to develop ourselves as loving individuals and disciples of Christ is to apply and practice empowering skills such as those discussed in this book. These skills will enable us to generate hope and strength against the power of fear and ignorance. They will help us increase our awareness and understanding of the underlying principles of successful human relationships. These principles are necessary for positive growth and will enable us to "live together in love."

Learning to Succeed at Love

The great human paradox is that we want love but we are not getting it. Parents want to know how to positively influence their children; couples want to know how to relate to each other meaningfully; teachers want more stimulating classrooms and better relationships with their students; and employers want more effective and trustworthy employees. Also, students do not want to be bad students; mothers do not want to fail as mothers; and fathers do not want to alienate their children. We do not want to fail and yet the pervasive evidence that we *do* fail is seen in escalating divorce rates, teenage runaway and pregnancy statistics, violent crime rates, and in the increasing number of suffering, fragmented families.

If people are by nature inclined to find goodness and self-fulfillment (and I believe they are), and if the Lord truly does want us to succeed (and I believe he does), then we might ask, Why are war, crime, alienation, greed, apathy, cruelty, despair, and unhappiness so prevalent? The answer lies partly in the unfortunate fact that in our society we *learn to fail*; we are conditioned to fail. We see so much negative, harmful modeling that we don't have clear ideas about what constitutes success and failure, and we experience great disparities between our ideals and our performance. Since optimum conditions for growth are rarely present, our capacity to succeed is often either neutralized or cut short.

Rising Above Externals

We fail because we have not learned to behave differently than we do; we have not learned to succeed . . . we don't know *how* to succeed. As a psychologist with years of counseling experience and as a life-long church worker, I have often wondered why there is so much mental and emotional distress among the faithful followers of Christ. I have come to the conclusion that too many are living their religion on a terrestrial level. They are loyal, responsible, and "active"; yet at the same time, they are judgmental, overly concerned with the opinions of others, and more concerned with rules than with people. They conform to external measures of righteousness rather than developing internal ones. To compound the difficulty, because such people appear to be doing everything right they may be placed in key positions of leadership, so we may mistakenly feel that they are examples of what we should be.

Seeing Possibilities Instead of Limitations

Though a just, dutiful life is vastly better than a hostile, violent one, people at the duty/justice level, like Joe and Carol Brown, always feel something is lacking—as if they are only getting "half a loaf." When they become aware of the excitement, renewal, and true joy of celestial living, they deeply desire it. The challenge is to break through the barriers of telestial and terrestrial living and focus on our options and possibilities, instead of our limitations. Celestial beings are full of light and truth, and they possess "a new heart and a new spirit." (Ezekiel 18:31.) Christ promised us that we, too, can become new through him and the redeeming power of his great Atonement.

Perhaps we have difficulty understanding and practicing love because we are confused about what loving people are like. We may think of them as weak individuals, do-gooders, or persons who refuse to face the harsh realities of life. Such is not the case. Loving people have learned to employ love in the toughest battles of life and to handle conflict far more effectively than those who have not learned this concept and its corresponding skills. In addition to tenderness, loving people have toughness and strength. They are concerned with outcomes.

Choosing to Live God's Greatest Commandment—to Love

Because loving people sense the divinity in all of God's creations, beginning with themselves, they have a spirit of fullness and harmony about them that is indeed beautiful. Loving people attract other loving people. Intelligence cleaves unto intelligence and wisdom cleaves unto wisdom. Truth embraces all truth. Those who project the strength and power of love attract those who are also loving, and they find deep satisfaction in such relationships.

As I define them, the eternal laws of love parallel the eternal laws of truth. The eternal laws of love are growth-producing, expanding, and unifying. They create win-win relationships. They create and generate trust and shared meaning through gift-giving, strengthened commitments, and oneness and harmony. They are the ways and power of love which not only help us grow but help others grow toward finding meaning in their lives.

The infallible guide to love is found within each person. At our deepest levels, we want to love and be loved. We want to be happy and joyful and to celebrate love in ourselves, in our surroundings, and with others. We want good things both for ourselves and others. We want to live on a celestial level and build love and trust in relationships and all of life.

Even though we may be physically mature adults with the potential to become truly honest with ourselves, we are often emotionally and spiritually immature. Paul reminds us that part of the growth process is to "put away childish things": "When I was a child, I spake as a child, I understood as a child, I thought as a child: but when I became a man, I put away childish things." (1 Corinthians 13:11.)

We can choose to remain on an immature level or to start on the journey of growth. We can meet the enemies—our own fears—and conquer them; we can learn to accept and embrace our *whole* selves, have the courage to look deeply within and show compassion to ourselves, and let go of our hostilities and protectiveness.

"For now we see through a glass, darkly; but then face to face; now I know in part; but then shall I know even as also I am known." (1 Corinthians 13:12.)

In this catharsis of spiritual amnesty, we can give ourselves the greatest gift of all: the permission and freedom to *grow* into perfection, remembering that even Jesus Christ himself was made perfect by what he suffered and experienced.

THE UNIVERSAL HUNGER

Jennifer, a vivacious young woman, is excited about being in her second year of college. She sits attentively in class, listening to Professor Lewis lecture about some of the great thinkers of the ages and the answers they have given to eternal questions and the meaning of life.

But after a while her mind begins to wander, and she begins to doodle on the edges of the paper. She finds herself thinking about her parents' divorce, which has left her feeling brokenhearted and confused. Since both her father and her mother seem to convey a sad emptiness, Jennifer does not feel she can find comfort in going to either of them. She feels distant from them and thinks maybe they don't want to be involved in her life at all. She wonders if she will be able to find a lasting relationship herself and hopes that she will not repeat her parents' mistakes.

Jennifer is attractive, bright, and intelligent. She feels confident about her studies and career goals, but she anxiously waits for some nice guy she met in class to call her. More than anything, she wants to be loved. Yet she wonders if the gospel principles she was taught as a child are anything more than nice-sounding ideas that don't actually work in real relationships.

Jennifer's teacher, Professor Lewis, has pursued the intellectual life for years, searching the writings of great minds for knowledge about life's certainties. Now, at fifty, he is respected on his university campus and has published two scholarly books. Although he enjoys a comfortable home and life-style, he is dissatisfied with a second marriage that has gone cold. Teaching is pleasant enough work, but often he would rather spend time with Eric, his four-year-old grandson, building toy rocket ships for journeys to fresh new worlds.

Looking back, Professor Lewis wonders why his pursuit of the intellectual did not produce the results he had expected. Though the framework of his life seems to be in place, he feels that something is missing. He observes that others appear to find peace in religious conviction, but he has always believed that religion is for the weak and dependent.

He is powerfully aware of Eric's meaning in his life, for in Eric he finds wholehearted acceptance and unconditional love. He realizes that peace is in the simple things that Eric, a child without guile or pretense, represents. In Eric's innocence, Professor Lewis finds a semblance of contentment, but he longs to experience innocence somehow again himself. Who else but Eric can understand the little boy still hiding beneath the beard and behind the glasses and framed degrees?

Jennifer's father, John, has been periodically inactive in his church for years; it has never been a powerful force in his life. At one time he was motivated by strong feelings to live Christian principles, but they were, after all, just principles.

For some years, he dragged his reluctant family from one place to another as he changed jobs, chasing the oil strikes. He worked long, hard hours to provide a living for his family. Then, when his father's death left him with an inheritance, John bought a home and a convenience store, and finally established some roots. However, John and his wife, Rose, soon became locked into regular arguments and disputes over how to run the business. When Jennifer, their youngest child, left for school, Rose decided she couldn't take any more and filed for divorce. A year later, she left on a Caribbean cruise for senior singles. Like John, she had never understood the real power of the gospel and Christ's message. Now she lives alone in the city and John lives alone in their hometown. They both wish Jennifer would write or call more often, and they both wonder if they can ever love again.

Jennifer, Professor Lewis, John, and Rose all long to be loved. The same is true of you and me and everyone we know. The child in the cradle, the retiree in the condo, and the single person in the classifieds are all looking for the same thing. Even the criminal and the insane want most of all to be trusted, liked, cared for, accepted, and loved. This longing to be loved is universal.

Our Journey

Cynics may believe that the destination of life's journey is death, but the real goal is love. Indeed, down deep inside, where our ideas smoke formlessly like underground fires, most of us believe that if we could just find love, the journey would be at an end. Then, with the searching completed successfully, we would enjoy a spiritual homecoming, a returning to the place we truly belong.

Poets and prophets of every age have praised love as the greatest and highest good. We see and hear about this elusive goal in popular songs, books, magazines, movies, and television programs. We all dream of love. Until recently, doctors and psychologists were hesitant to study love because it does not lend itself to the "scientific method" (that is to say, it is not measurable). But now, many in the helping professions acknowledge that loving, positive, personal relationships are essential to both physical health and mental well-being and so deserve our finest scrutiny.

Nevertheless, for all we hear, see, think, dream, study, and talk *about* it, we rarely *experience* love fully and directly. Instead, we experience, for the most part, the frustrations and illusions or counterfeits of love. And yet, each time we wake up disillusioned, we dress up and go out looking for love again.

Love is the most powerful force we can feel. Without it, life is never complete and never quite makes sense. Love alone gives meaning, power, and values that make an unjust and often cruel world worth living in. On the rare occasions when we do experience love, we know at a level deeper than understanding that it is the missing element of life, the essential ingredient that makes everything meaningful and full of purpose. Love is the power that transports us from a world of confused biological machines controlled by the environment to the realm of free and complete beings. Even the illusions of love can affect us profoundly, for initially they seem like the "real thing." That is the reason most of us would rather search for a new sham (though we do not know it is a sham at the moment) than give up hope and live in a world of anger, hopelessness, and pain.

The first of several reasons we fail to find the love we crave is that we think love is something we get from others. In fact, love is a *sharing process*, not a *receiving event*. If our hunger is ever to be satisfied, we must first learn to stop searching for love or for some-one to give love to us. Instead, we must seek to become loving.

Recognizing the Illusions of Love

We cannot obtain the goal of becoming loving people when we, in our ignorance, pursue love's counterfeits by "looking for love in all the wrong places," as one contemporary song says. Before we can learn to live a loving life, we must recognize the illusions of love for what they are so that we can avoid them. Let us consider some of the most common counterfeits of love and the faulty thinking that causes us to pursue them.

Illusion #1: Love Is Ownership

Although its intensity varies by culture, the idea that love is own-ership permeates the entire world. Popular songs often promote this clearly false and destructive notion with lyrics that may seem romantic, such as "You belong to me" or "Let me belong to you." The person who belongs to another is not a lover but an emotional slave. If we are not free internally, then we are lacking in "person-hood"; we cannot be loving in the fullest human sense. If we do not bring to a relationship a knowledge of our own value, we may well be simply looking for someone to take care of us.

Possessive love may look appealing because it seems to offer the type of security expressed in this thought: "If we belong to each other, then we can give each other constant assurance." This exchange might be called a contract to "validate each other's worth." However, no one of us is so emotionally stable that we can honestly issue assurance on demand. Such stability would be like being able to write checks on unlimited funds in a bank. If we try to do so, our affirmation soon becomes wooden and hollow, unfelt and unreal. Ultimately, one partner begins to question whether the assurance is genuine. This questioning feels worse than the insecurity that the possessive relationship was supposed to resolve.

Additional problems accompany this kind of thinking. Marriage partners are portrayed as being responsible for their spouse's happi-ness—a guaranteed formula for failure in a relationship. When we submit our personal worth to some other person, we lose control of our validation and value. Ownership quickly takes the form of control, and no matter how benignly it may be intended or how subtly it is used, resentment usually follows.

A newly found romance *may* give a thrilling sense of relief that the search for "my other half" is finally over. However, a possessive relationship may, in time, cause one partner to feel suffocated or "drained," while the other begins to feel burdened. The spontaneity that makes love so deeply appealing cannot survive in such a setting. True love flourishes with freedom and leads to openness, growth, and greater freedom. Love is *not* a "tender trap."

Illusion #2: Love Is Purchased

A variation on the "love is possession" idea is that we can exchange *things* for love. A young boy may trade candy or toys to gain entrance to a secret club. The adolescent girl may sell her body to gain acceptance. The rich, elderly man may promise his estate to a beautiful, younger woman if she will give him the only things he cannot buy, but what he wants most—attention and affection. In their desperate yearning, all three fall for the lie that love is for sale.

On the other hand, some people seem quite willing to sell their "love." Professional escort or massage services, known fronts for prostitution, openly advertise in most major newspapers. Others seek a more "respectable" route in the time-honored practice of marrying for money or power. Yet in every case, the truth comes out when the goodies are all gone.

Parents sometimes get caught in the trap of buying their children gifts instead of spending time with them. This way of buying love is easier to see and to stop than other ways because it is built on external, tangible things rather than internal values.

Illusion #3: Love Is Conditional

The illusion that love is conditional causes us to believe that we can earn love by doing favors, and pleasing and placating others. The roots of this belief may be in the socialization process in which children are rewarded for behaving according to their parents' desires. Though some of this socialization is necessary to maintain order in society, we need to teach our children that they are loved as individuals whether we approve or disapprove of their behavior at any one moment. Without this assurance, childhood can become a time of insecurity, a pattern which can lead to serious problems in adulthood.

Adults who believe love is conditional soon find themselves playing an endless number of pleasing games. They may feel like trained puppies, constantly on edge, afraid of upsetting the master, never able to relax and be themselves. They need to learn that in a loving relationship, people do make agreements to help the relationship work better, but they do not sacrifice personal integrity or deny their feelings.

Equating love with pleasing others, owning, purchasing, or meeting certain conditions presupposes that we can *trade* something for love. Loving is interactive, but it involves sharing, not trading or buying. It is "I and thou," not "this for that."

Illusion #4: Love Is Commanded

Another prevalent mentality is based on the premise that love can be commanded or forced—even that it *must* be. Thus, some husbands—even wives—unfortunately believe that what she (or he) really wants is to "know who is boss." A variation of this idea is that one proves love by "beating up" or chasing away real, potential, or imagined competitors for attention (as do stag deer, who compete in springtime battles to see who will dominate the females of the herd).

This "dominant mentality" can also be expressed this way: "I know we are meant for each other, and it's only a matter of time until you realize it too." This type of statement places the responsibility for the relationship on God, nature, destiny, or fate.

I once counseled a father who always dealt with disputes between his children by forcing them to embrace one another and say "I love you" before they discussed the problem. Convinced that he was following the commandment "Love thy neighbor," he could not understand why his children grew continually more distant from him and insolent toward one another

The key to understanding his problem is in the word "force." The father was trying, with sincere intent, to force the one thing that cannot be forced. The children of Israel were instructed in this way: "Ye shall not oppress one another." (Leviticus 25:14.) Even in the sphere of human emotions, the application of force always produces a counterforce. When the father tried to mandate love between his children, he was in fact eliciting an opposite emotion in his children: resentment.

Illusion #5: Love Is Macho Strength

Glamorized by the media in recent years, athletic heroes, renegade detectives, corporate raiders, and wealthy or promiscuous celebrities have come to represent the illusion that love can be equated with brute male strength and even violence. From *Rebel without a Cause* to *Dirty Harry*, the strong, silent type is portrayed as exciting and irresistible to women, a man who can capture their repressed gypsy spirits with one snarling, defiant, or arrogant glance. According to this description, the image matters most, not the real person inside, and the winner is the guy who maintains his cool at all times.

Others say winners must be cruel, if necessary, making all their important decisions in a totally rational, deliberate, goal-oriented manner. In this world of hardball and hard knocks, love becomes, at most, one of the spoils of war and, at the least, a palliative myth for sissies, losers, and children. Because of their fear of being ambushed in a vulnerable moment, these men behave in ways that deny them of their natural needs for openness, tenderness, and warmth. In their quest to prove their superiority and to exert control, they emasculate their own humanity.

Illusion #6: Love Is Feminine Helplessness

We see the female counterpart to this false standard in a syndrome that contemporary writers have called the "Cinderella complex," in which women think that in order to be loved they must be helpless and dependent. They believe that eventually they will be swept off their feet or rescued by a knight in shining armor (or a man in a Brooks Brothers suit) to be protected and taken care of for the rest of their natural lives.

More than a mere romantic notion, this modern fantasy becomes a literal mind-set for women who spend their lives waiting for "true love." This way of thinking is tremendously encouraged by the media's deluge of romance novels and television soap operas. A woman is led to believe that although she may be required to employ some duplicity to obtain her man, he will ultimately provide her with designer clothing and palatial surroundings, and will be emotionally available and supportive to her at all times. Typically, these modern heroes are handsome, unconventional, and aggressive, though they are not necessarily men of stability, character, and moral integrity.

In this way, dependencies are inaccurately promoted as love: a man thinks he must find a helpless female to dominate and control, and a woman believes her man must take care of her and provide for all her needs, as if she were a child.

Illusion #7: Love Is Suffering

Another widely held illusion is that love equals suffering. Cults, societies, and ancient religious orders committed to celibacy, poverty, or even self-torture have used these and other extreme deprivations to prove their love for a god or a cause.

Translated into contemporary terms the idea sounds something like this: "If I suffer sufficiently, I will prove to others—my spouse, my children, my friends—how much I love them," or "If I suffer enough, I will then be worthy of being loved by others." Such thought patterns generate guilt, perfectionism, and compulsive, self-defeating behavior and create victims, ineffectual leaders, masochists, and martyrs. Women may be especially vulnerable to such victimization. If they accept such illusions, they will eventually display a host of symptoms including emotional and economic dependencies, depression, and dependency diseases. Taken to the extreme, these conditions may develop into severe personality disorders, anorexia, or even suicidal tendencies.

Often these people are individuals from dysfunctional families in which one or more of the family members was controlling to the point of being a threat to other family members. Such suffering individuals learned to adapt in an unhealthy way to the real or perceived threat and became "codependent" on the aggressor and/or his behavior.

Originally a term only used in reference to the members of alcoholic families, "codependency" has come into popular use as a term that describes addictions recognized as emotional disease. John Bradshaw, who has helped others heal their own and family relationships, defines codependency as "a set of survival behaviors which are unhealthy patterns of learned behavior." He addresses the variety of ways in which "codependents try to make themselves indispensable by taking care of others . . . willing to do whatever it takes to be loved or worthwhile, even to the point of self-neglect."

When codependents assume self-sacrificing roles, such as caretakers and surrogate parents, they literally become enslaved by the illusion that their love is manifested in their suffering. They are vulnerable to abuse and often become victims who believe they deserve powerlessness and pain. They continue to sacrifice themselves and their well-being inappropriately, unaware of how clearly they are communicating to others that they are willing to remain victims.

The behavior of suffering individuals often does not communicate love to their children, spouses, or colleagues at all. Rather, codependents indirectly communicate that they themselves do not deserve respect and that they may be taken advantage of. They do not protect themselves emotionally or physically, and they magnetically attract abuse instead of love. In this way, codependents promote their own suffering by inviting others to continue to treat them like victims. They do not realize that love is not suffering. *Suffering* is suffering.

Illusion #8: Love Is Meekness

The concept that love is meekness is a milder version of the idea that love is suffering, and embodies similar elements. A common misconception among Christians is the idea that in order to love, one must always be nice, forever turning the other cheek, always going the second mile, and practicing the silent patience of saints. While the Beatitudes (or "beautiful attitudes") taught by the Savior represent Christian ideals to strive for, they should not be misinterpreted. According to James E. Talmage, a noted theologian, these illustrations of meekness in service to others "are not to be construed as commanding abject subserviency to unjust demands, nor as an abrogation of the principle of self-protection."

We do not become pure in heart by pretending to be a saintly person. A well-intentioned attempt to hide the churning heart, to show a placid face, and to be constantly calm, pleasant, and quiet forces our frustrations and anger underground, resulting in a denial of feelings and an artificial front. Jesus' anger was most quickly kindled by the religious hypocrites of his day whom he censured publicly for pretending to be what they were not. When he drove the money changers from the temple, he exemplified anger as a manifestation of love—or as we know it today, "tough love." This type of love is required when we must stand firm in preventing the violation of our personal boundaries or in communicating the need for appropriate respect. We must never get caught in the trap of allowing another person to manipulate or control us in the name of love (or meekness). Being "nice" may not be the appropriate or loving response to one who is attempting to manipulate, control, or abuse us.

Illusion #9: Love Is Electricity

The premise of many romantic novels is that love is a matter of physical attraction, often called "chemistry" or "electricity," and that it either exists or does not exist. Stripped to its bare essentials, "love at first sight," which supposedly occurs according to fate, denies free will in the most important area of our lives. It says that love cannot be learned or nurtured, but that it is simply a fact of cosmic destiny over which we have no control. Although spontaneous attraction can be invigorating and can motivate us to develop vitality in a relationship, it is not an essential element of genuine love. Further, no matter how high the voltage initially, the electricity always decreases in time and must be replaced by a greater, deeper, and longer-lasting stimulus. Some people will become addicted to the "sparks" and accompanying drama, and will continue to cross wires with even perfect strangers until they are electrocuted. They may live on a continual adrenaline high of charges and excitement in their relationships, but they never know the slow, quiet joy of true loving.

Illusion #10: Love Is Sex

Instructing the saints in Corinth centuries ago, the Apostle Paul plainly taught the concept of the sanctity of the human body: "Know ye not that your body is the temple of the Holy Ghost which is in you?" (1 Corinthians 6:19.) The people in Sodom and Gomorrah and the people who lived at the time of Noah were utterly destroyed for their wickedness and sexual perverseness. Now, as then, we are a society submerged in the insidious illusion that love is sex.

Our homes are flooded by an uncontrolled tidal wave of popular media including movies, magazines, and advertising, all of which promote the lie that love is physical beauty and sexual power. Highly staged and artificial scenes of utopian beauty and eroticism tantalize our imaginations and tempt us to pursue the promise of transcendent physical thrills. This process is aided by the great facilitators, alcohol and drugs, which effectively lower the body's inhibitions by producing temporary euphoria and the promise of more. Viewed by millions daily, television talk shows exhibit a major preoccupation with bizarre and deviant sexual life-styles and exploits. At the darkest end of this spectrum is the worldwide epidemic of incest and rape, and the proliferation of AIDS and other sexually transmitted diseases. These problems are growing like a cancer, destroying life and producing guilt and feelings of worthlessness which are damaging to the spiritual self.

A sexual union can be a manifestation of love, but loving sex is as much mental and spiritual as it is physical. Further, truly loving sex always takes place with a partner with whom there is emotional trust and involvement and whose flaws are known and accepted rather than covered by makeup, hidden by darkness, or removed by an airbrush.

The *Playboy* magazine philosophy was first based on the premise that the human body is natural and beautiful, and that it should be fully enjoyed by consenting adults. But it grew into a value system in which self-esteem is falsely dependent upon physical perfection and sexual prowess, and in which success is measured in terms of staying power, multiple orgasms, and number of partners conquered.

As the importance of technique triumphed over feeling, best-selling books on sexual skills poured forth. Pornography grew into a multibillion-dollar industry. Child pornography has skyrocketed, while X-rated film producers count on their latest releases to be outrageous enough to prompt publicity-generating confiscations and lawsuits. Pornographic publications and videos are readily accessible—even to minors. This deluge of sex largely ignores the human and emotional needs of partners. It has reduced love to mechanical performance and caused people to elevate sexual exploitation and gratification to a high-tech art, transforming degradation into a trendy, acceptable pursuit.

When sex is accompanied by love and practiced in accordance with God's rules, it is a natural and wonderful experience. Within

the parameters God has set, the combination of love and sex is one
of the finest avenues for deepening and expanding the dimensions
of a healthy marriage. An ancient prophet said it well when he
admonished his people to "bridle all your passions, that ye may be
filled with love."

Illusion #11: Love Is Marketing

The "Sell Yourself" school of thought would have you believe that
a potential mate or companion is, like you, looking for a bargain.
Therefore, a successful sale will be made only after you have prepared the product with careful grooming, stylish clothes, an effective
deodorant, the latest dance steps, and the mastery of a few great
opening lines. Then it becomes a matter of securing prominent display in dating clubs, trendy night spots, and various high-potential
social circles.

This process has always been celebrated in the world, from the
musical adaptation of the Pygmalion story, *My Fair Lady*, to the contemporary business marketplace, corporate sales, and professional
world. In the business and professional world, advancement and
monetary reward are achieved by those with the slickest, and most
convincing and attractive presentations that result in the highest
financial returns.

If we are immersed in this kind of daily life, our thinking automatically transfers to our personal relationships. The trouble comes when
we think we have to create an image, rather than be who we truly
are, in order to find love. The image divides us internally, making us
uncertain of who we are, consequently hindering our authenticity. At
the extreme, a marketing approach to love transforms us into hypocrites who cannot project what is genuine because we don't know
what is genuine.

Illusion #12: Love Is Worldly Success

The illusion that love is worldly success may be the advanced
version of an illusion that equates love with marketing skills and
success. When we come to believe the adage "Everybody loves a
winner," we believe that if we win at the competitive game of life,
we will be loved. People who actually believe this go to great

extremes to make their success obvious to others. If success has eluded them, they will employ creative, even devious measures such as surrounding themselves with the facades and trappings of prosperity, and acting suave and sophisticated in order to appear successful. Unfortunately, those who are caught in this trap may find themselves sacrificing their integrity or the quality of their family relationships to further their careers and to "keep up with the Joneses." This may seem to work for a while, and these people will attract potential companions who are along for a free ride. Once again, however, "love" developed in such relationships will be conditional and based on things.

Prosperity can be a positive experience, but we do not need wealth to be loving. Riches seldom bring happiness, as a well-known country song says:

How many times have you heard someone say
If I had his money I would do things my way?
But little they know that it's so hard to find
One rich man in ten with a satisfied mind.

There are many more widely held illusions of love, including the ideas that love equals worship, pity, duty, need, obedience, and so on. Like those mentioned above, these illusions are all capable of generating compulsive and artificial behaviors, and in time will only lead to an emptiness within. Even when everything else seems right, when all the necessary elements are in place, still a hunger persists when real love is not experienced.

What's Left?

After we free ourselves of all the illusions of love, what's left? Everything that matters! But what is that? If love is not something we own or which owns us, not something which we buy or sell, and not something which is commanded or submitted to, then what is it?

Love is many things—many of which cannot be expressed in words. But some of those that can be so expressed are discussed below.

Real love is the acceptance of self—right here, right now, including imperfections, warts, clay feet and all—knowing we are *in the process* of development and are not yet complete.

From this self-acceptance flows appreciation of others for all that they are, all they ever have been, and all they may ever become. They, like us, possess the greatest gift—themselves.

Real love is seeing the timeless giant within when the temporary littleness without is painfully obvious.

Real love is seeking the balance of heart, head, and body. Such a balance finds a working model that permits humility and teachableness—a "student forever" attitude. Such an attitude creates the ability to learn from all of life and to have an appreciation for all teachers, nature, family, and society.

What's left? Everything that fills us from within. Real love knows the difference between strengthening and weakening choices, and knows in the heart that life's answers and attitudes are indeed chosen consciously. We choose to have a life of happiness and joy or to allow ourselves to have a life of pain and unhappiness—regardless of external circumstances.

Real love knows that temporary agreement, comfort, and sympathy can be helpful or hurtful. Loving knows the traps of weakness and short-term payoffs and has the strength to pass up their alluring momentary thrills. Love does not ask the short-term question, "What makes me happy now?" Instead, it asks, "What will build my long-term capacity to deal with life effectively?" It demands high character.

Real love can confront and even eradicate the lies and games that destroy people, because loving fills needs before wants. Loving allows time and simple silence to work their wonders, and then speaks wonders when time and duplicity have made us ache for simplicity. There, in a whisper, love speaks: "What's left? The wellspring of hope."

Loving is knowing that the long road will end in unity and oneness, fulfilling the deepest and most natural desires of the heart. Loving is sensitivity to the furtive glance, the unplanned silence, and the breath out of rhythm. Loving is a state of deep trust and solid faith that tells you that inevitable conflicts can be resolved without anyone losing. Loving knows that anticipating the touch can be even more thrilling than the moment of contact. Probably there is no more beautifully or powerfully written description of charity, the pure love of Christ, than Paul's great sermon to the Corinthians.

But covet earnestly the best gifts: and yet shew I unto you a more excellent way.

Though I speak with the tongues of men and of angels, and have not charity, I am become as sounding brass, or a tinkling cymbal.

And though I have the gift of prophecy, and understand all mysteries, and all knowledge; and though I have all faith, so that I could remove mountains, and have not charity, I am nothing.

And though I bestow all my goods to feed the poor, and though I give my body to be burned, and have not charity, it profiteth me nothing.

Charity suffereth long, and is kind; charity envieth not; charity vaunteth not itself, is not puffed up,

Doth not behave itself unseemly, seeketh not her own, is not easily provoked, thinketh no evil;

Rejoiceth not in iniquity, but rejoiceth in the truth;

Beareth all things, believeth all things, hopeth all things, endureth all things.

Charity never faileth: but whether there be prophecies they shall fail; whether there be tongues, they shall cease; whether there be knowledge, it shall vanish away.

For we know in part, and we prophesy in part. . . .

But when that which is perfect is come, then that which is in part shall be done away.

And now abideth faith, hope, charity, these three; but the greatest of these is charity. (1 Corinthians 12:31; 13:1-10, 13.)

When we eliminate all the illusions of love, what's left? All we really want. Real love is being alive to the creative force of life, letting it flow through us, and being a free and joyous part of it. Love opens up the world, while hate and fear close it down. Love puts us in tune with ourselves, and with God and the universe, and makes us whole. Real love is seeing ourselves midway between the mysteries of the atoms and the majesties of the galaxies, and knowing our own mysteries are majestic, too.

And now . . .

Love is calling you by name, promising an end to the hunger.

So what's left?

Only your answer.

PART 2:
THE WAYS OF LOVE

THE FIRST WAY OF LOVE:
ACCEPTANCE AND AWARENESS

The first way of love is this: *Each one of us is unique and of infinite value. This value is enhanced by our awareness and acceptance of that value or worth. This value expands through the discovery and unfolding of our own individual meaning. This awareness and acceptance is the keystone to high self-esteem and to reaching our highest potential.*

Introduction: Finding a New Inner Reality

Henry David Thoreau said, "For every thousand hacking at the branches of evil there is one striking at the root." This book is about roots, not leaves and branches. Acceptance and awareness, the first way of love, can get us to the roots of who we are.

It is remarkably easy, especially in this society so impressed with the *appearance* of things, to get off track, to lose our way, to worry about leaves and forget about roots. We focus on style more than substance, and we believe that the image we create for ourselves counts more than the foundational character that undergirds worthwhile commitment and action. Believing that what we *own* counts more than what we *do*, or that what we *do* counts more than who we *are* often leads to nothing but self-doubt and uncertainty and the eventual conclusions that life is meaningless and that everything good is temporary.

However, secreted beneath all the temporary things of life there is a permanence, hidden and precious. Below all the noise of nature and civilization there waits to be discovered eternal identity and eternal realities that never change. We may not be able to vocalize these realities, but we know they exist. They are only discovered through awareness and acceptance of who we are, our divine origin, and our infinite worth. Beyond all the urgency of survival is a patience waiting for an awareness that is impervious to time. After all the words, pictures, symbols, and ideas have withered away, there stands a freshness, even an innocence, in the life-anchoring realization of our individual meaning. It is as new as it was before the universe first heard the command, "Let there be light."

This beautiful knowledge of our identity, our infinite worth, and the meaning of our lives is available to us in our most quiet, meditative, prayerful times, when we know we connect with this gift of light, when we know we are a part of God's vast plan.

The events of our lives are like a series of dances, and when each dance is over, the good songs linger, played by the private orchestra in the mind. However, there is one song that needs no mind in which to play—the certainty that we matter, that we are God's creations, that we are all connected to one another—that the light in each of us is the light in all of us. How do we come to know this song?

Sometimes when we read a great book or listen to a great teacher or speaker, we realize that our hearts and souls know that the words we are reading or hearing are true. Perhaps we, ourselves, cannot speak those words or express the feelings they bring, but often the poet, the novelist, the teacher, or the prophet can. And when we read or hear them, we know without argument or discussion that we are hearing the truth, though we have never heard it before in this life.

Perhaps we recognize truth when we hear it because we knew it even before our birth and because it seems familiar to our spiritual selves. Modern scripture and passages in the Bible indicate that we existed before this life began. Three of these are Jeremiah 1:15, "Before I formed thee in the belly I knew thee"; Job 38:7 (about the foundation of the earth before Adam), "All the sons of God shouted for joy"; and Ephesians 1:4, "[He hath] chosen us before the foundation of the world."

As the Bible clearly states, or at least implies, you and I have existed longer than this world has existed. In a way that our senses cannot comprehend, we, like the light fused into tiny rainbows when reflected from the facets of a polished diamond, have been shining longer than the sun. If this idea is accurate, we have a logical explanation for the inner knowledge in our heart of hearts of the truth

when we hear it—especially the truth about ourselves and our reason for being.

If we stand in the kitchen and peel away all the layers of an onion,
flesh and film in sequence, we will come to a green shoot in the center—the reason the onion grew. We may not understand the reason
for this growth, but we can sense the endless evidence of its existence. What is this mighty force that causes the onion to grow, to
become a white onion? Similarly, what causes a person to grow into
full personhood, into a full and whole human being?

There is a reason that anything exists at all and each human being
is a part of that reason. You are a part of that reason. That is why we
may start this discussion with the assertion that each of us is of infinite worth, we are God's children. We are connected to the source of
all life, and we are a part of all life.

That we are indeed of divine heritage is evident in the simple yet
deeply profound text of Naomi W. Randall's children's hymn, "I Am
a Child of God":

> I am a child of God
> And he has sent me here,
> Has given me an earthly home
> With parents kind and dear.
>
> Lead me, guide me, walk beside me,
> Help me find the way.
> Teach me all that I must do
> To live with him someday.

The psalmist asks, "What is man, that thou are mindful of him?
And the Son of man, that thou visitest him? For thou has made him
a little lower than the angels, and hast crowned him with glory and
honour." (Psalms 8:4-5.)

I call our eternal creator God, although others may use different
names: the prime mover, the Divine Mind, Holy Spirit, the logos,
the Tao, the flame of life, the infinite presence, the universal mind,
an old superstition, or simply "It." Though some even deny that God
exists, he is still there, an underpinning force in the life of every
individual.

We must each discover God in order to know who we are, here
and now. The insight that each of us is a child of God is the key to
self-acceptance and the ability to see the infinite value in every

human being. This is the cornerstone upon which all growth on the love/trust level is built.

At the core of each of us is our spirit, which is enhanced as we become aware of it and accept its divine origin. Here "enhanced" does not mean created, expanded, or even organized. Rather, it means revealed, allowed, explored, acknowledged, opened, tapped, unfolded, recognized, confirmed, found, forgiven, freed.

The first major developmental phase of living the love/trust life is recognizing the endless nature of our divine being. As we seek inner peace, we discover great insights about our eternal heritage and come to understand the Savior's offer and benediction, "Peace I leave with you, my peace I give unto you." (John 14:27.)

Accepting Our Uniqueness

While we all share a common identity as children of God, we are each unique in ways other than our biological characteristics. Since we are also members of the human fellowship, our personal value has both a general dimension—our common humanity—and a specific dimension—our individual uniqueness.

In order to examine the uniqueness that exists among people, I will use the example of my two sons. In addition to the commonalities that all humans share, my sons have a common parentage, home, culture, and so on. Their desires in life are generally similar: they both want to be good husbands and fathers, they both enjoy high self-esteem, and they both find fulfillment in their chosen fields.

In other ways, my sons display amazing contrasts. The younger one lives in the practical world and is always eagerly accomplishing visible, measurable tasks. He likes making things work; he is the "Mr. Fix-it" of the family. He loves the precision of numbers and excels in finance. A pragmatist at heart, he is not concerned with philosophy or theoretical consistency.

In contrast, my older son finds meaning in abstractions and ideas and loves to take part in complex discussions. He is a highly educated man and a skilled counselor, but he is not particularly interested in, or good at, the more practical aspects of life. Sometimes he would like to have more skills in money matters or in repairs, but his strengths lie elsewhere.

My two sons share similar general goals, but the ways in which they find meaning in life are very different. In a similar manner, we

often see discrepancies between the characteristics of marriage partners. Both partners may want to be good companions and parents,
and they may have similar goals and expectations, but choose their
own unique pathways to achieve those goals and to find personal
fulfillment.

Becoming Aware

The process of becoming aware is but another application of the
basic human valuing process: becoming aware of how choices forge
the future and then making strengthening choices. Balance is developed as personal integration, wholeness, and unity are realized.
These characteristics are achieved through the process of healing the
fractures within. When healing is accomplished, meaning and purpose become spontaneous and natural results of living, not external
things we obtain.

People living at the fear/anxiety level beg for meaning, communicate loudly, and hide or try to hide weakness behind a veneer of
bravado. This is because when the self is splintered or out of tune,
self-esteem is low. The various systems of personhood constantly
search for one another but rarely connect.

At the duty/justice level, the sense of meaning begins to emerge as
order replaces chaos, but this meaning is compromised for the sake
of "fitting in." Most often a person living at this level is still torn
between placating and actualizing. When we try to be real and
approved at the same time, frustration is the obvious result.

Meaning is highest in the love/trust life, but it is mainly expressed
in quietness, whispers, or symbols. The unified self shares quietly
and gently with trusted others, communicating with fearless eyes,
unhurried movements, and "good vibes." It's not that there is little to
say, but rather that most of what is to be communicated is beyond
the range of words.

The Human Valuing System generally defines attitudes toward the
world outside the self in terms of having, doing, and being; these
correlate with the three levels of living. We achieve these in certain
degrees, depending on our present level. When we live the fear/anxi-
ety life we feel judged by what we have and we judge others by what
they have; we judge the external shell only. As our shallow definitions become stereotypes, we limit growth by becoming trapped in a
myriad of narrow expectations.

At the duty/justice level, our perceptions of who we are and what we do often become intermixed. We develop self-definitions of loyalty, honesty, and reliability, and then prove these definitions by acting loyally, honestly, and reliably. This is all highly positive, but it is still an exchange on a surface level rather than a sharing of the core self. At the duty/justice level, we begin to see ourselves and others on a level that is deeper than behavior, but our insight is often blurred by continued expectations. This lack of clear insight tends to make our motivations and solutions weak.

At the love/trust level, we see and accept the inherent value of everyone, starting with ourselves. This unconditional acceptance provides a safe, nurturing environment in which everyone can grow. At this level, we say, "I am a person and I have value unconditionally. Others also have value unconditionally."

The more we see people at the core, the more accepting we are. The more we define people in terms of what they have or do, the more rejecting we are. Acceptance is empowering, rejection is weakening.

Entering a permanent "being" state of love, trust, warmth, care, compassion, and unity is possible. At this state, we have achieved fulfillment, self-actualization, and triumphant spiritual completion. We have found our own nature, what we most truly are. Though I believe it is impossible to achieve a perfection of this state in this life (within our limited, mortal bodies), progress toward it is what makes life joyful.

The answer to one single question will always put us on the main path for growth. The pivotal question that ultimately determines whether we advance or not is this: *Who is in control of my life?* Around the answer to this question, consisting of seven simple words, turns all the happiness of our lives. To say that this is the *central question* of life is not an overstatement. Loving people universally face this question squarely; uniformly they choose personal responsibility as the answer.

Defining Success and Failure

All this brings us to definitions of success and failure in human valuing terms. Success consists of being loving, caring, and trusting, and everything that accompanies these positive feelings. Failure is being fearful, anxious, hostile, and everything that accompanies these negative feelings. Notice that both are phrased as states of *being.* According to the Human Valuing System, success is a matter of internalized personal worth.

The purpose of the acorn is to grow into an oak tree. The purpose of the human being is to grow into all it can be. We can discover how far we have developed by determining the motives for our actions. Do we act because we "have to," "ought to," or "want to?" What makes our three favorite activities pleasurable? How many of the "ought to" items truly have to be done, and what is our attitude about doing them?

Your Marvelous System of Systems

Imagine who you are and what really goes on within you to make you function, all with no conscious effort on your part. Entire sets of systems function to serve you: the nervous system enables you to think; the muscular/skeletal system responds to your decisions for movement; the digestive system keeps all cells of the body supplied with energy; and the excretion system efficiently rids the body of waste. All of these systems operate automatically; no thought is necessary. When we do give them conscious thought, we realize the marvelous wonder that is this miracle we call a body.

Imagine further the brain's miraculous ability to perform mental imagery. Just through your imagination, you can picture objects and panoramas of events. When you read a book, watch the mental pictures the words bring into your mind.

Emotions, like visual images, are part of a real but unseen world; they have a powerful impact on us. The effect of a deeply spiritual experience leaves us transformed; the ecstasy of joy when we fall in love the first time can totally overwhelm us; the sorrow felt over the death of a loved one brings us grief, followed by the numbness required to survive that grief. As we look at our children, we feel grateful and experience a deep sense of wonder at our part in the creative process.

All of these emotions are part of this marvelous system of systems that we simply inherit. In addition, an understanding of our spiritual identity evokes a wondrous joy in its contemplation as our awareness increases of who we are—not of what we have or what we do, but *who and what we are*. If you know this one thing about yourself—who you truly are—you will know that you are valuable regardless of what others think. This is the very heart of the first way of love.

It is little wonder that the awareness of who you are and the acceptance of yourself stand at the very gateway of your entrance into the wonders and marvels of this world of love and trust. In other words, to discover meaning we must discover the self, which includes a conscious awareness of the individual being in its physical, emotional, intellectual, and spiritual aspects. To discover *who* we are, we must learn *what* we are. The key lesson to learn is that, as children of God, we are a marvelous system of interactive systems, all of which respond to the core or spirit self.

The Physical System

When we are students we learn basic anatomy, including the skeletal, muscular, digestive, glandular, and neural systems of the body. Unfortunately, the lessons on these subjects are rather blandly descriptive in most schools. For the majority of us, the awe and absolute majesty of the human body is not realized until we hold our first newborn child in our arms or suffer a serious injury or illness. We appreciate physical life most at those moments when it is given to us or when it may be taken from us. Even when injured, sick, or handicapped, love/trust people are profoundly appreciative of the body, and they use the abilities that they do have with wonder and joy. For example, many students at Gallaudet University for the deaf in Washington, D.C., are enthusiastic dancers. They can feel the strong bass tones and rhythmic percussion in their bones, even though they can't hear the sounds in their ears.

As we become love/trust people our senses become more keen. We notice the bird's nest in the landscape; we hear the intricate counterpoints in the music of the flute; we smell all the mysterious aromas of the forest; we taste the subtle herbs in a delicious soup; and we react ecstatically to loving fingertips lightly touching our skin. What we feel through our bodily senses is a source of happiness. We relish the physical beauty and amazing abilities of others, whether they be strangers on the street or world champion gymnasts in the Olympics.

Loving people tend to love their own bodies in an almost reverent way. They take an interest in good physical health, and they learn and heed the signals from their own bodies about what is good and what is bad for them. They do not abuse their finest gift with dangerous foods, chemicals, schedules, or excesses of pleasures. Neither do they see the body as a prison for the spirit, as inherently evil, or as something entirely separate from their mind or "real self." They recognize the crucial role which an open, positive attitude plays in bodily well-being, particularly in the resistance to disease.

The Emotional System

The connection between attitude and health demonstrates the essential gestalt nature of all the interrelated systems. Experts have now firmly established that crying and laughter are both therapeutic. Tears release toxins and tensions, and laughter releases the healing powers of the mind. This latter point is detailed in Norman Cousins' amazing account of self-healing in *Anatomy of an Illness*. Our physical and emotional conditions work together; the more open, honest, and real we are with ourselves, and with others when appropriate, the healthier and happier we are.

When we are in touch emotionally, we do not float on a still, tranquil lake but sail on a sea that sports frightening, stormy trials and beautiful sunsets of memory, pleasant vacation isles and terrifying depths of discovery. We experience fear and pain as well as confidence and joy and know that all these feelings, and many more, are part of the total experience of life.

The Intellectual System

In addition to the mind's power to heal the body, we have only the faintest understanding of many other limitless powers of the mind. We do not know what mental power enables fire walkers to enter a trance and walk barefoot calmly on white-hot coals. We do not know how Einstein, a man in his early twenties, could ignore all the limiting ideas gathered for centuries and choose instead to see and reveal many secrets of time and space. How do the yogis of the East learn to consciously control their hearts and respiration rates by thought alone? What abilities lie hidden within us, waiting to be tapped by hypnosis, faith, trial, or determination? Most importantly, how does the phenomenon of hope completely transform our inner world?

Even the most common accomplishments are miraculous when considered from a fresh outlook: How does a child learn all the intricacies of language and speech? People who spend their lives studying the brain and mind remain in awe of the most complex and elegant of all physical structures.

Most experts in the field believe that we generally use only a small percentage of the brain's capacities. Our intellectual system offers opportunities that are unknown and unfathomable at our current level of understanding. The human mind is indeed the last frontier; more mysteries await us in this inner space than exist in outer space.

Living on the love/trust level, we develop a penetrating admiration for the human intellect. We enjoy watching the growth of others and respect the views of those who have reached different conclusions than we have. We are careful to consistently feed and refresh our own minds with new ideas and new creations.

The Spiritual System

Using strong, supportive, "scientific" evidence, many people claim that intelligence, thought, and consciousness are purely the result of the brain's electrical action which evolved by happenstance over millions of years. Though I respect this position, I cannot agree with it.

When I see the hummingbird hang in the air, I cannot believe its grace and beauty are nothing more than biological tools for the survival of a species. When I see cracked, old hands, purple and misshapen, trembling in fervent supplication to a greater power, I cannot believe life is all in vain. When I stand alone on a mountaintop, I cannot believe that the uplifting of soul I feel is only the genetic remains of the lesson that there is safety on higher ground. When I think of people precious to me who have passed on, I cannot believe that their personalities were formed through a chemical process, nor can I believe that I no longer matter to them. The very nature of emotion and consciousness and the powers of the mind convince me that we are essentially eternal, spiritual beings. That God exists makes perfect sense to me; it "feels" right.

Spiritual awareness brings all our systems into balance and ties them together as one internal whole. If we will let this spiritual awareness mature naturally, it also becomes our connection to the external whole: society, nature, God's universe. Ultimately, our spiritual makeup is one with the Creator. Our spiritual identity is the force of life that animates our physical bodies, the spark of creativity that pushes the brain beyond its habitual thought patterns, and the source of our inner urges to be compassionate and loving. Spirit infuses our whole beings and unifies the body and the soul.

My deepest conviction is that we are literal spirit children of heavenly parents—spiritual creations that currently reside in physical tabernacles. "There is a spirit in man," Job tells us. (Job 32:8.) Numerous scriptures reveal and testify that we have been created by God in his own image, that we are only "a little lower than the angels." (Psalms 8:5.) The Apostle Paul further affirms that "we are the offspring of God." (Acts 17:29.)

Living the love/trust life means awakening ourselves to our transcendent spiritual selves. This spiritual awakening is most delicate and sensitive; because it requires great effort, it is seldom attended to by most of us. Physical exercise obtains certain results, but spiritual development is far more complex. Many achieve the appearance of spiritual aliveness, but their inward level of spirituality is hidden from other people. But when we do reach an inward spirituality, we know what it is and we love its taste. This spirituality enhances and magnifies all the other senses and faculties.

People hooked on running tell of the jogger's high—the euphoria that claims the soul when the body is pushed beyond its ordinary limits. People who have reached this edge of awareness feel new vistas opening up to them, and they can tell us about this transcendence. Those who experience transcendence in the emotional world experience, at times, a similar edge of awareness greatly magnified. Yet the balancing mechanism for all the others is the powerful but delicate world of spiritual transcendence where truly big things happen. We have marvels built into us that allow us a leap of faith.

Keeping the Systems in Balance

In order to apply the First Way of Love, we need to develop a balance between the physical, emotional, intellectual, and spiritual elements.

As we attain a higher consciousness, our emotional balance will actualize at the love/trust level of living. At that level, we realize that any virtue pushed too far can become a vice. We second the ancient Greek wisdom of Socrates, "Moderation in all things." We relate to Benjamin Franklin's lifelong prayer, "Oh, powerful goodness, help me to be true to my truest interest." And we join Ralph Waldo Emerson in asserting "the integrity of the human mind."

How Imbalance Occurs

The physical, emotional, intellectual, and spiritual systems interact in ways that may be positive, negative, or indifferent—balanced or unbalanced. For example, we might compensate for feelings of social inadequacy by pouring our energies into intellectual pursuits. Or we might be so intimidated by the "intellectuals" that we spend most of our time developing athletic prowess. We might learn to get our way by being charmers or flirts, consequently neglecting both academic and physical endeavors. Or we might choose to retreat into a mental realm of mystical dreams of other lifetimes and other worlds, and thus miss the opportunities provided by *this* life in *this* world. A compartmentalized method of living may bring success in the area of specialty we choose to pursue, but that success often comes at a high cost in terms of overall health and happiness. If we are to become self-actualized, we must find personal balance. Just as cars cannot run on one cylinder, neither can we be fully functioning human beings when some of our major needs are being starved so that others can be gorged.

The best athletes know that physical abilities make up only part of the challenge of their chosen game; they know that in order to be consistent winners they must master the mental part of the game, too. The charmer who has few intellectual or physical interests will soon be known as an airhead or a phony; he or she must be intellectually, physically, emotionally, and spiritually balanced in order to maintain credibility. Similarly, the truth seeker needs to find the truth of human love even more than the mystic secret, for learning to love is the purpose of this life, and joy and happiness are by-products.

People at the love/trust level are balanced; they have developed an instinct that tells them when and how to feed all four need areas in appropriate ways.

Correcting Imbalances

Barbara is an example of someone who is working toward becoming more balanced in the four need areas. Early in life, Barbara discovered that she was not as pretty as many other girls. This caused her great anguish through her teen years, a period of time when being popular seemed to be all that mattered. Like so many of us, she came to the illogical conclusion that she was not valuable because she could not measure up to the prevailing value scale.

After repeated failures at dating, Barbara decided to avoid more heartache by withdrawing from that arena. She created a private fantasy world by immersing herself in music. She studied piano, voice, and flute, as well as the history and theory of music. She even fantasized about living in the time of Tchaikovsky, a practice that helped her stop feeling melancholy. While she was in college, she performed in the orchestra. In this setting she found both refuge and expression, feeling comfortably hidden among a mass of musicians all dressed in black.

As time went on, her musical involvement inadvertently led her to discover her own value as she shared part of herself with others. As she secured work and recognition by performing solos at weddings and funerals, she became more confident with people and slowly escaped from her shell of fantasy. Though her intellectual and creative elements are still dominant, Barbara has grown dramatically in terms of emotional health and social relationships.

Because Barbara has become mature enough to understand her inner dynamics, she will likely begin to develop her physical characteristics as well so that her personality will be even more balanced. This development may come as she becomes involved in some activity such as aerobics, swimming, biking, or hiking.

In small, experiential steps, Barbara is outgrowing the illusion that her personal value comes from the approval of others. By taking action, she is learning that the only lasting source of happiness comes from within through self-acceptance.

Barbara's story is not unique. Similar stories could be told of people who have overemphasized the physical, the emotional, or the spiritual. It is not important what is emphasized and what is not. What is important is that such people experience a lack of balance. All four areas need *not* play equal roles; the goal is for each system to be sufficiently developed to meet the person's individual needs.

Examining Our Four Major Systems

To maintain balance, we must learn to listen to our inner reality. How do we learn to know the inner reality? The process is slow and gradual, although sometimes the speed of the process is increased by a great insight or a peak experience. We begin the journey within by examining each of our four major systems: intellectual, emotional, physical, and spiritual. We should observe and note our specific areas of interest and ability, and the relative balance between them. We can then make an inventory of our specific thoughts and actions that upset or improve the balance of these systems. We should also make a similar list of other people's actions and circumstances that can affect the balance of these systems. A rigorous self-analysis will greatly improve our awareness of this internal balance and how it can be improved. Simply becoming aware of and describing the process is our beginning point.

I often invite seminar students to diagram each of their major systems in a circle, drawing the dominating systems larger than the others. Students draw lines between the circles to symbolize the ways in which the systems affect one another. For example, I would draw my physical system a little smaller than the other three, and show that my spiritual needs often prompt intellectual inquiry. What makes this exercise useful is discovering the personal choices that feed or starve the various systems. People who seal their feelings inside themselves in silent boxes or drown in the tidal waves of uncontrollable emotions need to identify what words or actions initiate these processes. They need to outline the thoughts that lead to choices which are, in the long run, detrimental to their happiness. The understanding achieved through these steps can be the basis for developing a sensitive balance between the systems.

People who starve their intellect need to become aware of their alibi-creation and poor self-definition. They need to discover some intellectual interests that have natural appeal; these interests need not be some dusty academic subject. This awareness can be achieved by asking these key questions: First, what feeds your stronger systems? And second, where do you get your power and rewards?

Keeping Perspective

Focusing on Strengths—Not Weaknesses

Before we awaken to our own value, we are inclined to be obsessed with our flaws. But as we see and embrace our inherent value and that same value in others, we unlock a whole new dimension of potential. Once we see how much we have to work with, a boundless enthusiasm sets in. One who is self-accepting recognizes incongruities and puts them in perspective; the knowledge that these incongruities are temporary helps the self-accepting person to deal with them appropriately. Flaws do not become focal points but are patiently left in the shadows where they will likely disappear when the sun is at full height.

Too often people let weaknesses in certain areas limit their abilities in other areas. For example, the man who judges himself too short to succeed at basketball may think he cannot succeed at sales, either, and the woman whose voice is too high to be a TV news anchor may erroneously decide she cannot be a good teacher.

Some are haunted by the myth of Achilles, fearful that the smallest flaw will eventually prove fatal. Or, like the ancient Greek orator, Demosthenes, some believe that we will succeed only by focusing on infirmities and overcoming them.

However, Pericles, the major political leader in Athens in the age of Plato and Aristotle, provides a more apt example. He was born with an extremely misshapen head, yet historian Will Durant says of Pericles, "He was, as far as we know, the most complete man that Greece produced." He focused on his strengths; consequently so did those around him.

Some people not only focus on, but even feast on, the negatives and weakness around them. They blame society for its lack of solid values and complain about the screwed-up thinking of political and religious leaders. They bemoan the decreasing quality of life and confidently predict the ruin of civilization, using the daily newspaper as a source of supportive evidence. Yet people who blame the world for their own powerless position are really copping out. They feel that if they can blame someone else for their station in life, they are justified in failing to be responsible for their own lives. Rarely do they move beyond the complaining stage to draw up a plan for improvement and do something real to bring about needed changes. They believe happiness and control are external, since it is easier to believe that "It's all their fault," rather than to accept that "It's up to me."

On the other hand, those who value themselves develop their own strength. They foresee consequences of their actions and choose self-control, personal responsibility, honesty, and long-term growth.

This does not mean they have no problems or that society's negatives have no impact on their lives. But by choosing positive actions, these people deal with their problems directly. Love/trust people are not terrorized by conflict because they deal with it head-on.

At another level, we must deal with our weakness and find our strengths by searching our souls for the deep truths within us. This is something we should do in the privacy of a safe place. In a private place, we can give ourselves permission to cry aloud and to feel pain flow over and around us, unrestrained, as we look at pictures or memorabilia of a lost loved one, or of other times in our lives that caused us pain. We can listen to music that draws our deepest emotions to the surface so they can be healed. John Bradshaw said, "Healing demands the experiencing of the emotions. You can't heal what you don't feel." Writing down thoughts and feelings, though they may appear very random or negative on paper, may be beneficial. Whether in journal or symbolic form, writing is a tangible way of allowing ourselves to release feelings of inner pain, anger, confusion, or sadness. Such records of feelings also serve as ledgers of our personal progress as we become healed emotionally. Such a process is the wellspring of emotional strength.

We may find comfort and solace in searching the Bible or other scriptures, reaching for divinely granted grace and strength from a merciful God—a God who is aware of even the fall of a sparrow from a tree and each hair of our heads. Consider King David's many petitions to the Lord for peace and healing for his troubled heart recorded in Psalms:

> Therefore is my spirit overwhelmed within me; my heart within me is desolate. (Psalms 143:4.)
> O Lord my God, I cried unto thee, and thou hast healed me. Weeping may endure for a night, but joy cometh in the morning. (Psalms 30:2, 5.)

Consider also the strength of David's testimony:

> I waited patiently for the Lord; and he inclined unto me, and heard my cry. He brought me up also out of an horrible pit, out of the miring clay, and set my feet upon a rock, and established my goings. And he hath put a new song in my mouth. (Psalms 40:1-3.)

Each of us can develop that same strength.

Keeping the Big Things in Control

Suppose that Dr. Dale is late to the office because his car was rear-ended in a traffic jam. He rushes in, cursing under his breath. He tries to hide his anger from his patients but they sense he is upset and assume that he doesn't like them. Dr. Dale would tell anyone, on a good day, that the big things to him include a good working relationship with his staff and a clientele of satisfied patients. But at this moment, he is letting a little thing, a minor accident, take control of the situation and threaten the success of the big things.

Julia will say that trust and security between her daughter and her are big things in her life. However, when three-year-old Amanda interrupts Julia's phone call by running into the house screaming that the little boy next door is beating her up again, Julia responds by yelling at her daughter, "I told you not to interrupt me when I'm on the phone!" This response communicates to Amanda that her mother doesn't care if she gets beaten up. An irritating interruption has taken control over what is really important to Julia.

Singer Jackson Browne phrased it this way: "Sometimes we forget we love each other and we fight for no reason." Or we might paraphrase his idea this way: "Sometimes we forget that love is the big reason and we fight for little reasons." The truth is that we often let little things take control, which keeps us from focusing on the big things that are important. The big things include love and trust, comfort and caring, honesty and respect. The little things that stand in the way include pride, irritations, money, and tight schedules. Instead of allowing relationships to control the issues, we allow issues to control our relationships.

People who are working to develop a love/trust life learn to recognize key moments when the little things threaten to take control. They learn how to stop this process and keep the big things in control.

Being Sensitive to Timing

In Ecclesiastes 3:18, one of the most well-known passages from the Bible, King Solomon records this poetic insight:

> To every thing there is a season, and a time to every purpose under the heaven:
> A time to be born, and a time to die; a time to plant, and a time to pluck up that which is planted;

A time to kill, and a time to heal; a time to break down, and a time to build up;

A time to weep, and a time to laugh; a time to mourn, and a time to dance;

A time to cast away stones, and a time to gather stones together; a time to embrace, and a time to refrain from embracing;

A time to get, and a time to lose; a time to keep, and a time to cast away;

A time to rend, and a time to sew; a time to keep silence, and a time to speak;

A time to love, and a time to hate; a time of war, and a time of peace.

This passage is a classic statement that says everything has a proper time. Love/trust people develop an intuitive sense of timing, and they do not hesitate to seize the moment. They detect hidden clues that someone needs to be listened to, and they sense when listening should best be delayed or when the present time must do. The key to this timing is being sensitive to people's feelings and level of understanding.

As a young scoutmaster, for example, I believed it was crucial for the boys to know that I loved them. To express this love to them, I lined them up and said, "I want you all to know that I love you very much." I'll never forget the nervous looks I got from that ragtag bunch of twelve-year-olds in reaction to my words.

After working with the boys for six months, I learned to send messages that were more appropriate for their level of understanding, and my timing and language improved. Instead of saying, "I love you," an awkward expression for boys at that age, I would slap them on the back or kick them gently, and jokingly say, "You aren't too bad" or "You'll probably make it after all."

At times, the statement "I love you" can elicit a reaction of distrust and distance, for instance when "sweet talk" is used to avoid or end an argument. Big, important words can become little and hollow when they are used at the wrong time. Later, if the distrust has dissipated and a preliminary bedrock of trust is reached, the same words of caring can have a profound, penetrating effect. The essential point to remember is that when we are trying to allow the big things to be in control, timing is as important as understanding the idea itself.

Choosing Wisely

As we mature, we see that the world offers us a myriad of actions, values, and beliefs from which to choose. Sometimes we must choose between opposites, but more often we must choose from a range of possibilities. Most of us find that deciding on our own way of valuing can be dizzying at times.

If we try to follow all conventional wisdom and pay indiscriminate heed to the advice of others, we will only be torn apart by "all the winds that blow." When operating at the love/trust level, we learn to stand quietly in the eye of the hurricane of advice because we know that our solutions will flow from the calm within rather than from the wild winds whirling around us. This statement does not mean we should be unteachable or closed minded; rather, it means that our search is not frantic because it is based on the certainty of our own value and the goodness of life in the long run.

This same principle applies in our efforts to follow the advice given in the scriptures. Many deeply religious people who want to follow every word of scripture find themselves thrown into painful paradoxes. They read that "the well need no physician" and conclude that they should go among the sinners to do their work. But they become confused when they then read the warning to avoid the appearance of evil. (The key to unraveling the many paradoxes found in the scriptures is knowing when a line or a verse applies to a specific situation and when it applies in a larger context.)

Paradoxes also occur in other areas, including literature, politics, music, philosophy, and popular culture. For example, the adage "Look before you leap" fits many situations and its apparent opposite, "He who hesitates is lost," fits many others. Neither adage will fit all situations.

Though eager to learn, when we are on the road to self-actualization, we are not gullible; we resist arguments that are forceful only in form or faddish in content. Our search for wisdom in the form of traditional information continues throughout our lives. Sometimes we have heard enough of what others think and we just want to be alone with our own thoughts. We learn, most of all, to trust the voice within.

Reading Your Inner Compass

As we learn to read our own inner compass, that intuitive and internal system will send us warning signals when we get off the mainstream of growth. This skill is a boon, because when we go off on tangents we waste time and become frustrated. The compass swiftly acts to keep us from going off track. In many ways, our progress toward the loving life is measured by how quickly and accurately we respond to danger signals and get back on course. This whole process leads to an efficient use of our life energy, a force that is often squandered when we wander in the woods instead of following the path.

When we are at the fear/anxiety level, our compass is unreliable because its messages become entangled with strange desires of self-destruction and retaliation against others. At the duty/justice level, the pointer is more trustworthy because we are oriented in the direction of the positive values of honor and fairness. However, these virtues are sought mainly by external conformity, so that indications of our compass are sometimes shallow. When we are at the love/trust level, our inner sense of rightness is highly reliable because it is reacting faithfully to the most congruent and positive forces within us: a vivid respect for personhood and an unfeigned hope for human success.

The following story illustrates these ideas. Two business partners split up their partnership amidst great bitterness, each accusing the other of being insensitive to his needs. For several months, they carry on a vindictive argument, each building a case to show that the other is wrong. This bitter debate gives each of the partners immediate rewards in the blood-pumping thrills of revenge.

Slowly, one of the partners begins to feel that something is missing from his life, that the acrid dispute has become a slow-acting venom, deadening him from within. At first, because of his pride, he does not want to hear these messages that come from his inner sense of rightness. He is obsessed with winning the battle. However, the tones ring persistently, for they are harmonics of his own true self. As he tunes out the static and listens to the music of his soul, he hears the lyrics clearly. They tell him that belligerence only lowers self-esteem. Soon he understands that he cannot afford the personal effects of all the negativity and that he must make a positive change.

As a result of this decision, he starts to change his feelings, to let go of the faultfinding, and to begin the long process of finding a resolution with his former partner.

The inner sense of rightness can be highly creative if we will only allow it to work, and it is the most sure source of inner peace.

Cultivating Humor

When we are at peace within, we live with a naturalness that is often light in mood. When we are confident of our own worth, we can take kidding without feeling threatened. We can even find delight in poking fun at our own peculiarities.

We can develop the real skill required to use humor to get rid of a tense mood without creating winners and losers. The surest way to relieve this kind of mood is to gently snicker at one's own quirks, appreciating the fact that simple, human foibles can be very funny.

Seriousness is sometimes needed, but it often needs to be relieved with a good chuckle. However, we also need to remember that our world's definition of humor is anything that makes us laugh, from a silly play on words, to a heartless guffaw in derision of another's frailty. Sometimes an entire audience will erupt in the sick laughter that makes a scapegoat of an innocent person. People at the love/trust level are offended by such sacrifice and do not join in the jollity. They know when "laughing with" passes into "laughing at," and they know that respect for others is worth more than any joke. Their abstention is not some self-righteous or deliberate snobbery; rather it is a natural reaction to an inner sense of rightness, the compass within, which leads to an inevitable consideration and acceptance of others.

Accepting Attitudes

Accepting Others

Unconditional acceptance of ourselves and others is one of life's most difficult, but nevertheless necessary, prerequisites to developing full, rich, wholesome relationships. Learning how to value someone more than their behavior is not easy. We are so accustomed to living in a world that assigns worth based on "what you have" or "what you do" that it is odd to even think of value being based on "what you are."

Yet this unconditional acceptance is at the root of creating the trust that is the foundation of lasting solutions to interpersonal conflict. Usually we expect others to measure up to our image of them, and often they try to—faithfully playing out the script we hand them. This creates an atmosphere in which people are simultaneously trying to please and be pleased by acting out roles. However, if the roles are not natural, we can maintain an impersonation for only a limited period of time. Eventually, we must pull off the masks and breathe free, or else suffocate our souls. This is because if we are not honest in our actions, we will die within. So many people are so frightened that their true selves will be rejected by others that they reveal their inner selves only in their dreams, in prayer, or to a diary.

Imagine for a moment the powerful feeling of completely revealing your real self to another person without fear of rejection. Imagine that this being is perfectly full of love and understanding— a being who can take in all flaws, insecurities, fears, embarrassing blunders, painful disillusions, and buried dreams and desires, and still say to us in total honesty, "Yes, you are accepted. Yes, you are beautiful." Jesus is the perfect example of such love and He gave a new commandment, "That ye love one another; as I have loved you." (John 13:34). That is charity—the true love of Christ—an unconditional love based on the inherent worth of the soul.

Acceptance Invites Trust

We are all aware of our own lack of ability to love everyone unconditionally, and we need not be *perfectly* accepting to be a safe place for someone else. The desire to open up and share without the fear of rejection is so deep that most people will reveal themselves whenever a listener is even *trying* to be accepting. Even when we fall far short of this ideal, any efforts at all to be unconditionally accepting will improve our communication with others.

Consider the mother who believes and has taught her children that teenagers should not be sexually active before marriage. Her sixteen-year-old daughter has recently become quite distant, and is behaving suspiciously. If this mother is earnestly trying to practice unconditional love, instead of initiating a campaign of lectures, scripture quotes, and snide comments about other girls who get "in trouble," she will say, in complete honesty and at appropriate times, things like, "I may not agree with your choices about how to live your life, but I want you to know that I see you as a young lady able to make her own choices and to be responsible for them. I know I could not control you even if I wanted to do so. Most of all, I love you for yourself, as my daughter and as a human being, no matter what you do. I need you to know this." By so doing she is safeguarding her ability to influence her daughter, and keeping the big things (honesty, trust, and the warm flow of openness and warmth between them) in control by seeing the inherent value in both herself and her daughter. She maintains her position of being a safe place for her daughter to come.

The ability to be accepting of another, independent of that person's behavior, comes slowly to most of us and is the result of a long series of insights and lessons learned from seeing the results of our judgmental relationships.

When unconditional trust is established we feel safe. Gone are the secret "hooks," the "strings," and the dreaded "Catch-22's." With such conditions done away with, we can relax and be ourselves without fear of judgment or rejection. This allows us to open up, communicate, and share personal feelings. We can then speak from the deepest core within and reveal our most keenly felt intentions in ways that are real and sincere.

Influence Versus Control

In this setting of safety and acceptance, we cannot have "control over" one another. Instead, we have something far finer: "influence with" one another. Influence is superior to control because it invokes changes that are motivated from within rather than from without. Yes, changes wrought in this more subtle way are likely to be slower in coming than those brought about by outside control, but they are far longer lasting because they become part of the person, not just part of the moment. Further, to have "influence with" shows a thorough respect of the free choice of others. In a practical sense, this means that we refuse to use force—physical, economical, or psychological force—on any other person. Mental force in the form of withholding love and approval is probably the most common form of force. When we develop a love/trust attitude we are aware of the long-range destruction that these methods produce and are willing to learn and practice more productive ways of dealing with conflict.

We choose to retain "influence with," by respecting others' freedom of choice. Influence is not resisted as is control or force. Influence is free of unrighteous dominion.

Once we feel safe in such an environment, we can honestly express our opinions to one another and thus have accurate data to work with as we approach our common problems. In contrast is the protective or artificial information we give when we feel threatened. This difference is one of the key reasons that solutions based on trust last, while patchwork answers, based on fear, do not last.

An interesting thing happens when we learn to approach our conflicts in an accepting way. In the warm light of total acceptance, many problems melt away like icicles in the spring sunshine. Why? Because many of our differences are just layers of motionless air we have wrapped about us as insulation from the cold winds of judgment. Of course, not all differences disappear easily, but we often find that many of our differences exist only in our perspective or in our choice of words. In many other cases, we differ not so much in what we want as in how we go about getting what we want.

When we finally decide that a relationship matters more than our disagreements, then an air of acceptance will lead us to a foundation of trust. Solutions can then be built that avoid all the wasted energy of playing games and saying one thing, doing another, and feeling yet another. Feelings of unity replace conflicts of disparity.

Many people will say that they believe in being accepting and try to do so. But often what they really mean is something like, "I will accept Berta after she changes her behavior and earns my approval." This is a circular statement that makes no sense; it is putting the cart before the horse, for acceptance must be given unconditionally. If Berta is accepted only *after* she has changed, then she will never change for the right reason and she will never change enough to "earn" the acceptance of the one demanding that she change. Consider the following statements that communicate acceptance: "It's true that I don't like what you've done with your time this year, but I respect your right to decide" or "I don't like what happens when we fight like this, but it's worth it to me to keep trying to find solutions. I really want to find a better way."

The power of acceptance can be invoked only when we recognize people as valuable regardless of their behavior. With that foundation principle established, if we feel the need to offer an honest statement about annoying behavior, we will do it in a way that separates the action from the worth of the person.

Accepting Yourself

If we could listen in on the thoughts of someone who has reached the love/trust state, we would hear the expression of a series of choices, values, judgments, and attitudes that would sound much like the following:

I have deep and personal value. This value lies both in the things I share with all other humans in the world and in the things that make me unique in all the universe.

I allow myself the freedom to be completely me. I will creatively express myself in ways that work for me. My life's purpose is to discover and make my meaning real. Narrow self-concepts limit this growth.

I have dignity and see dignity in all others. However, my respect is balanced by a sense of humor, which allows me to enjoy "popping my own sillies" but will not laugh in a way to diminish someone else.

I am a marvelous system of systems. The physical, intellectual, emotional, and spiritual aspects of me don't always agree, but I allow them all to be active, and I feed them all. Sometimes one system is dominant, but the systems are generally in balance. I am an interdependent whole, and I am part of a larger interdependent whole.

I value my gifts. My body is a wonder and I care for it. Only a few parts of me exist that I do not share with anyone. I am real and I am not ashamed of my tears, my happiness, or my sadness. My spiritual aliveness does not need to argue, nor will it be bullied. I know when I am on track. I can feel when I am on a tangent, and I get back on track before I make a serious error. I live in an imperfect world. Being part of it, I know that I am imperfect too; but that is just fine for now. I know my strengths and my limitations. My clay feet are okay, and I choose to amplify my abilities, not merely to overcome my weaknesses. I have an inner sense of rightness, and I trust it. My intuition is at least as powerful a guide as my intellect. I respect both.

I am responsible for my own growth. My happiness is my job, and I cannot and will not assign it to anyone else.

My past is not a chain that keeps me in tow, but a rear view mirror that helps me maintain my direction on my current road. I have earned the present. What I am right now is the result of all my past decisions. I have a right to use all the options open to me.

The only person I can control is me.
The only time I have is now.
I value my own life.
I respect life.
Knowing the risks, I choose to love.

The Acceptor's Choice

When we develop attitudes such as these we know ourselves and gain a permeating sense of peace from that knowledge. Seeing that freedom is the result of self-discipline, we remain committed to self-control; but it is the self-control of a calm will, not the self-control of a clenched fist and gritted teeth. We recognize personal prejudices and neutralize them. We identify old cop-outs and rule them out. We pass up the quick thrill of the nifty plan and quick fixes. We are patient with ourselves and other strugglers. We know from experience how hard it is to be loving while living in a fear/anxiety world. Yet we love anyway. Perhaps the crowning paradox of acceptance is this: It is the total opposite of resignation. Acceptance is a conscious decision to be a harmonious part of the flow of life. Acceptance means not giving up, but living up.

Acceptors are the chosen people. That is, the people who have chosen. They have chosen the Christlike life, not just the facade of conformity. They have chosen to center control in Christ, as did St. Francis of Assisi who said:

Lord, make me an instrument of thy peace.
Where there is hatred let me sow love;
Where there is despair, hope;
Where there is darkness, light;
Where there is sadness, joy.

Oh Divine Master, grant that I may not so much seek
To be consoled as to console;
To be understood as to understand;
To be loved as to love.

For it is in giving that we receive;
It is in pardoning that we are pardoned;
It is in dying that we are born to Eternal Life.

THE SECOND WAY OF LOVE: SELECTION AND ORDER

T he second way of love is this: *As we increase in self-esteem, we select principles, concepts, and skills that strengthen and enhance us in a larger context. We reject weakening attitudes and behaviors and intuitively know the criteria by which to assess success and failure. We consistently make the choices that allow us to become active, self-correcting people.*

Introduction

The Bible says of Jesus: "Though he were a Son, yet learned he obedience by the things which he suffered." (Hebrews 5:8.) We, too can learn to live in harmony with law from the things we suffer. The path of progress is one of constant improvement and self-correction.

The first way of love—acceptance—is largely a matter of self-esteem: knowing, being, and liking ourselves. Through acceptance we integrate the outer self with the inner self and find personal congruence. The second way of love, selection and order, is built upon the first.

We first experience an inner awareness, and then we reach out to select supportive answers from the world. As those answers are internalized, a new urge arises in us, an urge for outward form and expression. Knowing, feeling, thinking, and talking are no longer enough. The impulse for growth pushes us out, demanding us to take action.

It is a matter of the unified self reaching outward to find or create a corresponding harmony with the world outside. The first way of love involves a search within; the second way of love involves a look without, a decision to make choices to align our lives with eternal laws—to live the principles we have learned.

Choosing to Change

Our uplifting insights and stirring personal revelations must be coupled with new skills. We need practical ways to make the ideal work in the real world so we don't get caught in our old traps as soon as challenges come along. We need to establish healthier habit patterns to sustain our higher awareness.

In this transition stage, we are practicing, as would a young musician learning to play an instrument or a doctor or lawyer gaining practice in performing their respective professions. When we first learn the skills of the Human Valuing System, they feel awkward and mechanical. We may feel as self-conscious about our efforts as the novice musician. But as we become more able to make selections, the skills become natural, integral parts of our personalities.

Following Physical and Spiritual Laws

Just as physical laws of nature exist, so do laws that describe human interactions. However, unlike inanimate matter, people have the power to make individual decisions, so the laws that describe human relationships do not describe human behavior in absolute, defined terms. Instead, they outline general patterns of behavior and expected reactions. Similarly, the laws of social science describe the behavior of large populations in terms of norms and deviations.

These laws of social science have been used to organize civilization and to free us from the bondage of chaos. However, that freedom is for society as a whole. If we are to enjoy that freedom individually, we must organize our own lives and be disciplined enough to cooperate with the order of the world.

As actualizers, we are aware of these physical, social, and spiritual laws and we accept them gratefully. We do not rebel against these laws, but learn them, conform to their self-evident truth, and feel at peace as a result.

Though the laws of human behavior are less clear and harder to define, they nonetheless do exist. These laws give each of us a practical meaning so that we can make sense of it all. We understand that when we take action that brings negative reactions, we should not be surprised that we are unhappy. We also understand that when we cooperate with uplifting forces, we will gain the natural reward. This is why freedom is not the result of indulgence, but of discipline.

Freedom is impossible without discipline. To be fully expressive we must have a foundation of order. A creative teacher may have the enthusiasm required to inspire his students, but he will not be successful unless he is in class on time every day, gives assignments faithfully, grades papers promptly, and completes all his practical duties.

Thinking for Ourselves

In the second way of love we learn that the responsibility for forming a set of beliefs is ours alone. We must select our own holy wisdom book and interpret it in our own terms. In this way general principles are not held hostage to the fallibility of individuals.

The young need heroes and rewards because they have not yet developed the ability to choose which principles to adopt on the merit of the principle alone. But placing allegiance in people rather than principles is dangerous. For instance, suppose we wish to emulate a famous athlete, and then discover that he is a drug user, and by association, lose confidence in the sound principles of consistent training. Or, we may lose faith in the principles that a church leader teaches when we discover that his actions do not always measure up to his words. Whenever we see a person as the embodiment of a certain tenet and attach our loyalty to the person rather than the underlying principle, we are likely to eventually become disillusioned.

As we mature, our faith should shift from the externals—such as heroes, rewards, and security symbols—to internals. As we establish our own foundation of principles, we should start by defining our own personal values.

Healthy, enlightened adoption of principles comes as we evaluate the long-term benefits of the principles themselves rather than placing importance on these principles because of the personal charisma of those who teach them

The next major lesson is that bad intentions are not usually our problem. Generally, we all want to succeed. Our failure patterns from the past can be unlearned. Moving from a fear/reactionary attitude to a dutiful orientation is a giant leap forward. However, even this leap is dwarfed by the birth of the belief that we can actually become open, trusting, and loving people.

In seeking answers to the enigmas of life, many of us have been asking the wrong questions for so long that we don't even know how to shut up, wake up, and learn from the obvious. For example, in a situation of conflict our immediate reaction is to prove that we are right and the other person is wrong; we want to cast blame and impose punishment.

Such actions are unthinking, automatic, and hurtful because blame and punishment rarely lead to solutions. In fact they usually make the situation worse by further dividing people who need to work together. Blame and punishment often bludgeon self-esteem out of existence and create recurring feelings of self-righteousness or revenge. And yet so many times we choose to follow these negative patterns again and again, never considering the price we are paying or the benefits we could get by choosing to avoid such behavior.

We need to seriously question old ingrained habits. As actualizers, we do not choose to repeat actions that we know don't work, all the while living "lives of quiet desperation," as Thoreau said. Instead, we use our ability to foresee the future because we choose see the consequences of our current choices. We remember Abraham Lincoln's example, when, in the midst of his pain caused by the Civil War, he pointed out that the ways of the past were outdated and useless, and that bold new ways of thinking and acting were needed.

Finding Simplicity Beyond Complexity

While speaking of the perilous times of the last days, Paul said that some would deviate from the straightness and simplicity of the gospel into divers perversions—that they would be "ever learning, and never able to come to a knowledge of the truth." (2 Timothy 3:7.) This is the pattern we must avoid.

As small children we lived in a simple world. We found intense joy discovering all the wonders of the world. Happiness in childhood consisted of being loved, being fed, and having fun. Most of our learning occurred naturally through rewards, punishments, and natural consequences.

As we grew older and ventured out into the neighborhood, life started to get more complex and less rosy. We started to learn, in

shocked surprise, that some people didn't like us. Some of our play-
mates were bullies, some snobs, and many of them were stingy or
selfish.

As time went on, our plans fell through, our knees got scraped,
and our hearts got broken. At times we decided that life was just too
hard, and we became either hostile and demanding or withdrawn
and submissive. As we learned that neither of these behaviors
brought back the simple pleasures of earlier days, we began a life-
long search for either an answer to our problems or an oblivion—a
way to escape from our problems instead of dealing with them.

However, our search for knowledge often brought more confusion—for the more we learned, the more we knew how much we
don't know. In our personal lives the more we experienced, the more
we found out how many of our actions did not give us the results we
wanted. Yet we were inclined to keep repeating these actions anyway. The longing for a solution grew deeper. Some people who quit
searching for an answer may fall into the oblivion of dementia,
drugs, or death. Many slip into a comfortable apathy. Perhaps a slight
majority keep searching.

As we choose to become actualizers, we learn that the only way
to find our way through the maze of life is to make our own decisions and to be responsible for and love ourselves. We find that love
is the basic answer to our problems: it is love, which starts with
accepting oneself and expands into accepting others, that heals and
makes life worth living. Only through this awareness does the
frightening confusion of the world give way to a new simplicity.

Accepting Responsibility

A young woman I once counseled discovered this to be true. This
young woman was attractive and personable and had plenty of leadership skills. However, something was missing in her life. She had
an intense desire to be happily married and have children. Sometime
after her thirtieth birthday, when she was fearful that her childbear-
ing years would pass unfulfilled, she came to me complaining that
her life was worthless. In addition to being frustrated with the dating
game, she was angry at men, herself, and God.

For a long time, I listened to her complain and express her pain.
Eventually, I saw that listening was not enough, so I started to confront her with valuing questions. "When you blame men, yourself,

and God, for your position in life, does that make your situation better or worse?" She agreed that it made it worse. Then I asked, "Even though you are not a wife and mother, are you worth something?"

Her response was definite. "Yes, I am. I am a good person and a competent professional. I care for people and they care for me."

As we focused on her personal worth, her self-esteem and attitude underwent a transformation. The fog of excuses she used to explain why she was still single slowly lifted, revealing a woman who was self-contained, one who wanted to share her life with a man but did not need to do so. In fact, early in life she had decided to do what was the right thing for her, to secure herself a worthwhile, successful life even if she did not marry.

She followed my suggestion that she start concentrating on the simple basics of life and take care of her own needs first, and then serve others. As she developed this new attitude, she could allow herself to relax on dates as she could never do before. She lightened up and let her inner happiness shine through. She quit asking herself each time she went out whether each date was "the one," and she stopped evaluating each man's every move against her "ideal man" standard. Within a few months, a couple of men had become interested in her, and six months later she married the right man for the right reasons. It was by making a definite move into the love/trust level of living—not simply by getting married—that she began to live a much more satisfying, enjoyable life.

As we learn to make our own decisions in a loving way and to be personally and solely responsible for our own lives, every decision from that point is affected. We obtain a sense of power that simplifies life. We find pleasure in our families, in work, in personal relationships, and in nature. We no longer try to please others or defeat them; we simply find meaning in what we believe and desire. We know what works and what doesn't, and we know that trouble can be dealt with positively. Once we have found the truth within ourselves, we no longer need to spend our lives looking for it elsewhere.

Because of our new love/trust level awareness, we know that if we select principles of self-defeat, we will be shut off from the possibility for growth. Knowing we do not want that, we no longer accept ideas just because they are "in style" or recommended by someone else. New ideas and old ones must measure up to the following valuing standard: Will the effect of my decisions in the long run make me stronger and more responsible for my own life or make me weaker and more dependent on the approval of others? Being actualizers, we know the difference between the addicting quick fix and the patient and strong commitment—the commitment that includes the knowledge that cause and effect are always connected.

Understanding the Rules of Cause and Effect

Some believe that our ability to understand cause and effect, to visualize and foresee the future, is one characteristic that separates us from lower animals. According to this view, only humans plan and prepare for the future by planting crops, saving money, and so on. Animals that seem to prepare (beavers building dams, squirrels hiding nuts for winter) are in reality acting purely out of genetic instinct, and not from conscious awareness. Animals, like small children, have a consciousness that sees only the current moment.

Like animals and children, many of us continue to live according to genetic and cultural instinct, elevating destructive habits to the level of instinct. We sometimes neglect to utilize our consummately human, almost divine, power to form the future in our own best self-interest. We say we understand the power of choice, but sometimes act as if we don't. We sometimes consider only the immediate results of our choices, like children at a carnival who eat one cotton candy after another for the immediate pleasure, oblivious to the headache, grumpiness, fatigue, and tooth decay that may follow. A child may be largely ignorant of cause/effect relationships; in contrast, a grownup may choose to deliberately ignore or deny them (for example, consider the person who knows the dangers of tobacco smoking, yet continues to puff away).

Why, when we are free, would any man choose a lower path? Why would we enslave ourselves to the *tyranny of the moment*—the short-term but harmful quick payoff—as if we were infants with attention spans of twenty seconds? Why would we refuse to claim our human birthright, the godly power to create the world we want to live in right here on earth? Only lack of awareness of a better way could explain such a decision. But the cost of ignoring our godly power is monumentally tragic and is measured in millions of wasted human lives. Even Christ lamented, "How often would I have gathered thy children together, even as a hen gathereth her chickens . . . and ye would not!" (Matthew 23:37.)

The results of our choices are inevitable, and just as negative results come from negative choices, good results occur when we "pay the price." For example, we cannot obtain the result of trust by asking for, demanding, or begging for it. If we want the result of being trusted, we must first choose to behave in trustworthy ways.

Through our new awareness and new commitment we can make the quantum leap in human maturation to grow in the second way of love. We can overcome the habitual numbness of the mind and spirit that deadens the awareness of so many. We will no longer think of the future in an abstract, detached sense, as if it were something that will happen *to us.* Instead, we see our future as something that we will bring about and *cause* to happen. As actualizers, we take an active role in our own lives. We *choose* to positively influence and control what happens to us.

As we develop the second way of love we choose to be responsible for our lives by clearly visualizing nature's cause-effect laws of human nature. Our desire is to make all our choices in favor of our own long-term self-interest. The central idea here is "long-term." Time perspective is the issue. When presented with a choice, at the love/trust level we identify all our options, evaluate them according to long-range effects, and choose the best one. Though this process sounds remarkably simple and obvious, few people practice it consistently. (Many young people rarely think of long-term consequences until they practice for an important athletic event or see the results of sloppy class work on a poor report card.)

Because most of us believe there is life after death, another powerful question arises—a long-term question that we must all answer: "For what shall it profit a man, if he gain the whole world, and lose his own soul? Or what shall a man give in exchange for his soul?" (Mark 8:36-37.)

As actualizers seeking long-term rewards, we know how to forego the thrill of the moment and its accompanying short-term gratification to do what we must in order to get what we truly want. We know better than to sell our birthright for a mess of pottage.

This valuing principle that keeps us on course for the long-term rewards we most want has several names: one is sacrifice—the giving up of one reward for the sake of eventually gaining a greater one. Another name for it is investment, the putting away of money and making it unavailable for current consumption in favor of future, more satisfying availability. There is a cost, but there is a reward too. Though we cannot immediately spend the money that we save, we can eventually do big things with it—buy a home, educate our children, make plans for retirement, and experience the wonderful pleasures and confidence of a self-reliant life. Another name for the principle is the law of the harvest, whereby we plant the wheat instead of eating it, and later harvest an increase of a hundredfold.

Gaining a Long-Range Perspective

I call this long-range selecting power "ultra natural" rather than supernatural because the principle that says "deferred consumption yields exponential results over a period of time" is one of the most fundamental characteristics of nature. We see this power in the way the laws of nature work—for example, the gestation process during which human mothers must suffer physical discomfort for most of the year to bring forth new life. This ultra natural power is simply the inexorable result of time and patience well spent, the knowledge that great gifts take time to incubate before they can be born.

The Human Valuing System says simply, spend your time well, for the results are irreversible. Use your consciousness, your free choice, the laws of nature, and your mind to free yourself from the tyranny of the moment, to escape the human paradox, and to find freedom, including the freedom to follow correct principles. This is a freedom that leads to peace within and relationships that work.

William James, the founder of American psychology, said the following on the subject:

> We are spinning our own fates, good or evil, never to be undone. Every smallest stroke of virtue or of vice leaves its ever so little scar. The drunken Rip Van Winkle, in Jefferson's play, excuses himself for every fresh dereliction by saying, 'I won't count this time.' Well, he may not count it, and a kind heaven may not count it, but it is being counted nonetheless. Down among his nerve cells and fibers, the molecules are counting it, registering and storing it up to be used against him when the next temptation comes. Nothing we

ever do is, in strict scientific literalness, wiped out. Of course this has its good side as well as its bad one. As we become permanent drunkards by so many separate drinks, so we become saints in the moral, and authorities and experts in the practical and scientific spheres by so many sets of acts and hours of work. (William James, *Psychology*, Henry Holt & Co., New York, 1892, p. 120.)

We all want freedom, the increasing ability to be who and what we are. In seeking this freedom, we cannot look for only the short-term payoffs; we must also consider the long-term consequences of our actions. We must value ourselves enough to make sacrifices. When we are training for a race or trying to lose weight, we cannot eat mounds of fluffy sweets, say we will make up for it the next day, and then expect to successfully reach our goals. When we address the issue of long-term human *fulfillment* (not survival only), we must realize that real human success involves much more than externalities. The peace and progress of the inner person are of prime importance.

As we move to the love/trust level, we overcome the weakness of looking for short-term payoffs. We develop the vision of time that is so distinctively human but too often remains dormant or weak. Because we learn that the world we see is largely a matter of what we choose to see, we begin to choose positive attitudes because we want to see the world in a positive way.

Using Selective Perception in a Positive Way

We are constantly bombarded by information from the outside world, but we train ourselves to notice only a small percentage of it. We are surprised when we listen to one of our conversations that has been recorded and discover how much background and irrelevant noise we filtered out that the tape recorder picked up. Most of us would likewise be surprised to see a candid photo taken of the interior of our houses that shows the books in the corner or the streaks on the window that we never notice anymore. The process of subconsciously and consciously choosing to notice only certain parts of our environment is called *selective perception.*

Because we can't cope with all the information we come in contact with, we learn to filter out all but what we need or want to receive.

What we decide to perceive, what we notice, is our world. Thus by learning, choosing, selecting, editing, and filtering, each of us creates a private world.

Attitude is a key factor in determining what we see, or in other words, how we create our world. For example, some people believe that "you can't trust anyone." Such individuals allow this notion to define their world; eventually, the belief becomes a self-fulfilling prophecy. The more suspiciously they treat others, the more surreptitiously others react to them. On the other hand, if we select the attitude that people are trustworthy, we will find those in the world who want to be trusting and trusted. Believing in trust is harder, though, because it requires that we learn to risk. In order to build trust we have to make and keep commitments, and at the same time avoid gullibility and game playing. We must risk more to build a better world. Love is truly for the strong, but everyone can develop some degree of strength if they choose to. The rewards are well worth the effort. There is a definite cause and effect relationship: when we choose an attitude, we also choose all the life-changing effects of that attitude.

If we can choose any attitude and live in the world that this attitude creates, why then would anyone choose a life of fear and distrust? Only because they don't know how to behave any other way. It is not evil nature or intent, but ignorance and fear that are actually our great enemies. The ways of love teach us how to overcome those enemies.

Learning from Our Heritage

One popular notion says that we come into the world with nothing and that we leave it in the same situation. Though we do enter this world helpless, innocent, and naked, we also arrive with a noble birthright. Part of this birthright consists of a heritage of civilization—the traditions that our ancestors established to slowly lift themselves out of chaos—and the institutions that give us a choice of places and stations in life. Most of this heritage is a boon, a gift of incalculable value to be honored and passed on. But some of this heritage is a curse. The commandment to "Honour thy father and thy mother: that thy days may be long upon the land which the Lord thy God giveth thee" (Exodus 20:12) does not mean that we should continue to accept and believe everything we were taught in our youth.

Separating the helpful elements of our cultural heritage from the debilitating ones is part of the selection and order process. This selection is sometimes clear-cut, the helpful elements being clearly superior to the hurtful ones. But often the good and bad elements are not so well defined. Thus, sometimes we must ask: "Will such a selection bring about growth toward self-control? Will it weaken or strengthen me?" Our challenge is to make practical sense of all the confusing and contradictory messages we receive. When we make conscious choices and decisions, we know that if we make bad choices, we will inevitably pay a price, and that if we make good choices, we will receive a payoff.

Recognizing False Beliefs

If we never see the light about the long-run impact of our choices, we may slowly go blind in spirit believing ideas that seem to be good for us but that are in fact harmful. Here are some of the more commonly held beliefs—part of our cultural heritage—that result in *long-term negative results*:

1. Love means having no arguments.
2. Crying is a sign of weakness in a man.
3. Arguments should be avoided by ignoring our problems.
4. Success is having lots of fancy clothes and neat things.
5. Mom or Dad really knows how to handle a man/woman/kids. (Occasionally this is true, but it is rare.)
6. I will be happy when I grow up/ get married/ finish school/ get a raise/ get the kids married off/ lose weight/ retire/ go to heaven, etc.
7. Humans are by nature evil, contemptuous, selfish fighters. Expect the worst and you won't be disappointed.
8. Why worry? *Que será será.* (Whatever will be, will be.)
9. It doesn't matter what I do, my fate is set by nature/ the stars/ karma/ justice/ God/ genetics/ the economy, etc.
10. Predestination is the answer: only the elect can qualify for God's heaven, and all others are doomed.
11. Success is survival and only the ruthless survive.

The self-actualizer looks at each of these values and the many others common in our culture and asks: Does this idea, over the long haul, produce growth, enhancement, and movement, or does it produce closure, deadness, and rigidity? Does it increase self-sovereignty or does it encourage dependency?

Gaining Strength to Be Who We Are

Though the self-actualizer likes to be part of the group, he or she will not compromise personal integrity to gain popularity. If we have determined certain ideas from our cultural heritage are wrong, we will stick by that determination. As we become selectors, we are our own drummers, and though the beats may be soft and low, we know that the rhythm of that music is sweeter than any reward we could receive from following the roar of the crowd. As selectors (individuals who make moral decisions), we are strong enough to allow ourselves the freedom to be exactly who we are. Though we will quickly admit and correct a mistake, we do not beg for the approval of others by apologizing for our beliefs, avoiding personal responsibility, making excuses, or blaming others. We are committed to learning and choosing those behaviors that will strengthen us in the long run.

Often it is upsetting to identify our beliefs and then discover that they are actually harmful to us, because our beliefs provide us with a support system to live by. When we discredit beliefs that we have held to for long periods of time, we feel unprotected. We can patiently deal with this insecurity by giving ourselves the time necessary to develop a new support system. The corroded support beams should be removed gingerly. Each weakening idea that is discovered and rejected must be replaced by a new, stronger one.

The thoughts and attitudes of someone who is selecting the positive elements of his her heritage would sound something like this:

We know that some of the values and ideals of our culture are wrong because they tend to cripple the human spirit. When we can distinguish between myth and reality, we can make more intelligent choices.

Choosing Harmony

The practice of choosing—a rational and deliberate process at the duty/justice level—evolves into a natural response at the love/trust level. In addition, intuition is so sharply honed that it becomes objective. The explanation of this apparent paradox is simple. Our culture generally teaches men to be left-brained, "straight-forward" thinkers who concentrate on dissection, detail, and sequence, and it encourages women to be right-brained "round" thinkers who emphasize holistic, spontaneous, and creative thought. Regardless of our gender or the way we are taught, we simply cannot be whole and function with only half of a brain. The self-actualizer understands this and works to help the suppressed side manifest itself.

As a result of the ability to use both sides of the brain, the person at the love/trust level recognizes when unity is decreasing and when division is developing, and knows how to respond. The person at the duty level also feels this way but doesn't know how to remedy the situation. When one-sided thinking begins, the self-actualizer responds to correct the dissonance and will naturally reestablish harmony in his life and bring the song of the self back into tune.

How can we learn to develop these skills of harmony? We must begin with a heightened awareness, which we can develop by asking ourselves this question: "What closes me down?" Typical answers include cop-outs, prejudices, labeling other people, evasiveness, and so on. After we determine what closes us down, we need to catalog what choices open us up and make us more teachable and less fearful. Typical answers might include slowing down long enough to smell the roses, telling a story of a long journey to someone who is truly interested, and sharing a new and happy discovery with a friend.

Choosing Strengthening Behaviors

We feel good when we make decisions that move us toward the love/trust life; we want to experience those good feelings more often. To do so, we cannot bumble through life imitating the models we saw as children, which in most cases were fear/anxiety models. Neither can we follow the example of those who try desperately to buy their way out of negative patterns. These people get caught in the trap of the cheap thrill or quick pleasure, and end up emotionally bankrupt because they have purchased so many emotional "bargains."

As we move to the love/trust level, we learn to recognize that all these "bargains" are really of poor value, and we choose, instead to pursue quality, which in the long run is much cheaper.

The Commitment Process

In the Human Valuing System, the skill that "makes it real" is commitment. Choosing strengthening behaviors always requires commitment. When we become committed to choosing strengthening behaviors, we find a bedrock of trust. After we find this bedrock, we then move through several stages, asking ourselves these questions: First, what is going on and what do we want? Second, how would we like things to be? Third, what can each of us do to reach our common goals?

Commitment requires that we center control in ourselves and that we allow all of our cop-outs and blaming tendencies to come to their natural dead ends. We agree to be responsible for what we can do and not for what others should do.

The next step is to anticipate the problems that will occur. Every improvement plan is going to run into roadblocks when it is tried out in the real world. It is important for us to foresee problems, when possible, and to preplan ways to solve them.

After we discover what our general goals and anticipated problems are, we need to identify our specific plan. If the goal is a family or group goal, we need to determine who is going to do what and when. We need to decide when we are going to have a meeting to evaluate results, and what will be the standards of measurement (if determining these standards is possible). Clearly placing responsibility is a powerful way to move from the thought to the deed.

Actualizers use this commitment process both with themselves and others because it gets the job done—and avoids doing too much thinking or talking and not enough doing.

Myth	*Reality*
• The love of money is the root of all evil.	• The worship and pursuit of money strictly for its own sake corrupts people.
• Violence proves one's power or masculinity.	• At certain times physical force may be necessary.
• Romantic love is an exquisite helplessness.	• Romantic love must be nurtured from a natural seed.

Myth	Reality
• Those in authority must be obeyed even when they are wrong.	• We must follow leaders we can support by free moral choice.
• If there's a winner, there must be a loser.	• To achieve teamwork and accomplishment, sometimes we must compromise to find solutions to human conflict.

Avoiding Analysis Paralysis

A trap awaits people who think about their problems too much. It can be a way to procrastinate making a commitment, making a choice, or moving forward. In *She*, H. Rider Haggard says, "Thinking only serves to measure out the helplessness of thought." Thinking through a problem is good, but one can do too much of a good thing. We can get so bogged down with this type of thinking that we never come up for air and end up with a case of analysis paralysis. As a result, nothing practical is ever done about the problem."

This type of bogging down happened to my oldest daughter when she was in college and was trying to decide whether to run for an office in student government. She became caught in a cycle of "what if" questions because she wanted other people to decide for her, to show her that they approved of her by pushing her into running for office. When she finally asked herself why she was having such a hard time making the decision, she found that she was afraid of losing the election, afraid of losing friends, and prestige, and that she was afraid of looking foolish. Locked into approval-seeking, she thought, "What will others think of me if I lose?"

Eventually, she decided to take the risk. She broke out of her analysis paralysis and joined the race. The campaign was marred by a couple of ugly incidents, but she handled them with maturity. In the end she lost by a small margin. She knew she had made considerable effort, but she was prepared for the loss. After releasing some tensions through tears and sharing her feelings, she let go of it and put the incident aside. A week later, she was back to her natural, bubbly, warm self. She chose strengthening behaviors.

Strengthening Behaviors in Relationships

Using our personal strength development for our criterion, we replace momentary "solutions" with a positive approach to relationship problems by asking questions such as the following:

1. What is going on between us?
2. What will happen if we continue to act as we have been acting?
3. Is this the result we want?
4. What do we really want?
5. What do we do that divides us?
6. What strengthens and what weakens our relationship on a long-term basis?
7. What can we do to get what we want that will result in both of us winning and in a strengthened relationship?
8. What helps us come to trust each other more and what erodes the trust we have already developed?
9. What helps us open up to each other, and what causes us to withdraw from each other defensively?

Asking the above questions will help us recognize and avoid unproductive ways of meeting interpersonal conflict. The following conflicts are the most common:

1. *Choosing up sides, creating bonds with or against others.*
   - Immediate reward: Feelings of support, loyalty, belonging.
   - Long-term result: Divisiveness. Time and effort are wasted on conflict rather than invested in teamwork.

2. *Giving sympathy.*
   - Immediate reward: Soothing of and justification for feelings.
   - Long-term result: Avoiding the issue at hand, a weakening of problem-solving abilities.

3. *Deciding who is right and who is wrong.*
   - Immediate reward: Being right feels good and we begin to determine who can be trusted (or who is like us).
   - Long-term result: Division, alienation, and other barriers are created, and energy goes into fighting one another rather than solving the problem.

4. *Giving advice.*

- Immediate reward: A good feeling that comes from help-ing someone in need.
- Long-term result: If the advice works, the advice-seeker returns for more advice and develops a dependence on us; if it doesn't work, the advice-seeker blames the advice giver. (Either way, the advice-seeker avoids responsibility and the advice-giver is caught in one trap or another.)

5. *Running (we retreat, complain, sulk, cry, withdraw).*

- Immediate reward: Escape from threatening situations.
- Long-term result: We become emotional cowards who avoid conflict and miss opportunities for growth that can come from dealing with conflict productively.

6. *Fighting.*

- Immediate reward: A winner and a loser are designated, and a "settling of the score" occurs.
- Long-term results: More divisions, battles, and a determina-tion to "even the score," locking us into a fear/anxiety life.

7. *Ignoring.*

- Immediate reward: The relief of believing that there is no conflict.
- Long-term result: We feel a numbness or internal fracturing as we try to convince ourselves of a lie or become deadened to the reality of the need for choice.

8. *Intellectualizing. (I am not making a statement against being thoughtful and thorough. I am making a statement against using analysis as a form of ignoring the real issues and the need for action.)*

- Immediate reward: Comfort that comes from the belief that understanding a problem solves it.
- Long-term results: We smoke screen the real issue. We may become internally phony or lose touch with our emotions. We concoct solutions but never get past the theory stage. We experience paralysis that is a result of excessive analysis.

Listed below are unproductive but commonly used questions people ask when they are experiencing conflict:

1. Who started this fight?
2. Who is to blame?

3. Who is right and who is wrong?
4. Who do I agree with?
5. Who is loyal and who is disloyal?
6. Who is "in" and who is "out"?

Each of these questions is divisive and builds barriers rather than bridges between the people involved. Each causes us to focus our strength and energy on "fighting" other people rather than solving the problem.

The Savior's Pattern for Relationships

Notice the great contrast between the answers to those questions and the advice from the Sermon on the Mount which models all the ways and power of love:

> And seeing the multitudes, he went up into a mountain: and when he was set, his disciples came unto him: And he opened his mouth, and taught them saying,
>
> Blessed are the poor in spirit; for theirs is the kingdom of heaven.
>
> Blessed are they that mourn: for they shall be comforted. Blessed are the meek: for they shall inherit the earth. Blessed are they which do hunger and thirst after righteousness: for they shall be filled.
>
> Blessed are the merciful: for they shall obtain mercy. Blessed are the pure in heart: for they shall see God. Blessed are the peacemaker: for they shall be called the children of God.
>
> Blessed are they which are persecuted for righteousness' sake: for theirs is the kingdom of heaven.
>
> Blessed are ye, when men shall revile you, and persecute you, and shall say all manner of evil against you falsely, for my sake. Rejoice, and be exceeding glad: for great is your reward in heaven: for so persecuted they the prophets which were before you.
>
> Ye are the salt of the earth: but if the salt have lost his savour, wherewith shall it be salted? it is thenceforth good for nothing, but to be cast out, and to be trodden under foot of men.
>
> Ye are the light of the world. A city that is set on an hill cannot be hid.
>
> Neither do men light a candle, and put it under a bushel, but on a candlestick; and it giveth light unto all that are in the house. Let your light so shine before men, that they may see your good works, and glorify your Father which is in heaven. (Matthew 5:1-16)

In addition to this earth-changing advice, the Savior challenges the very nature of the way human beings react to one another:

> Ye have heard that it hath been said, Thou shalt love thy neighbour, and hate thine enemy.
>
> But I say unto you, Love your enemies, bless they that curse you, do good to them that hate, you and pray for them which despitefully use you, and persecute you;
>
> That ye may be the children of your Father which is in heaven: for he maketh his sun to rise on the evil and on the good, and sendeth rain on the just and on the unjust.
>
> For if ye love them which love you, what reward have ye? do not even the publicans the same? (Matthew 5:43-46.)

As we internalize the Savior's words, we can continually build greater and happier relationships and learn to live on the love/trust level more and more of the time.

A Loving Perspective of Self-Interest

This second way of love, selection and order, includes learning to make all our choices with a loving, appropriate perspective of self-interest. We choose strengthening behaviors because doing so is in our best interest. We are sometimes taught that it is wrong, even sinful, to think of ourselves first, and that it is better to give than to receive. This idea ignores the natural, basic human motivation: to find out "What's in it for me?" In spite of the values society teaches us, the Human Valuing System is based on the truth that the only reliable, consistent human motivation is self-interest. To say that such a blunt statement of human nature is part of the law of love may seem to strain traditional belief. Yet, as we have previously discussed, the two great commandments, "Love the Lord" and "Love thy neighbor as thyself" are contingent on first loving oneself.

The nature of self-interest changes as we become more healthy. At fear/anxiety level, self-interest is manifest as deceit, selfish indulgence at the expense of others, and as a desire to defeat others. At the duty/justice level, self-interest is manifest as fairness. Thus, those at this level decide that it is in their own self-interest to be fair with others if others are fair with them. Those at the love/trust know that we need each other and that cooperation is better than competition. Love/trust people are committed to win/win relationships.

People who accept themselves are not selfish. Selfishness is manifest when someone gets personal rewards at the expense of another in an attempt to find personal value in overtaking or undermining things or people. Such an attempt may increase one's net worth, but it will not increase self-worth. On the other hand, once someone develops personal worth within, there is no need to feign this worth or to seek substitutes. The most self-accepting individual is the least selfish.

As we place our own needs in perspective and fulfill them without feeling guilty, we learn to place other important priorities in perspective, too. When we are living the fearful life, we let little problems, such as traffic and taxes, control us and take away our warmth and caring. When we are living the dutiful life, we strive to balance opposing forces. When we are living the trusting life, we pursue major goals instinctively and fulfill small but necessary needs without a second thought. At this highest level of living, we develop a proper hierarchy of needs and proper hierarchy of values.

We give higher values more importance than lower values if we will allow ourselves to be led by love. As we learn to do this, we will undergo a metamorphosis. I have attempted to show the change from the secret, inner beginnings of love to the solid manifestations of it around us in this chapter. In the chapters that follow, we will discuss the outcome of this inner growth as it is supported by invigorating ideals and exercised in the real world.

THE THIRD WAY OF LOVE:
INTERNALIZATION AND
CONFIRMATION

T he third way of love is this: *As we internalize our highest personal values and the principles that produce growth, a deeper confirmation of the true self occurs. The need to have or possess gives way to the need to be. The larger self quietly and lovingly begins to control the lesser self, and the fractured self meshes into a unified whole.*

Introduction

The deepest of all human needs is to feel valuable; we all need this assurance. However, we tend to hang on to the labels of inadequacy we received in childhood. Probably all of us are somewhat flawed from our childhood, when parents, teachers, and other children gave us negative labels, such as "fat" or "foolish" or "flighty." If we continue to carry those negative labels around with us, attempting to live according to the roles defined for us by others, we pay the fearful price of never realizing our true selves.

If I know that I count, that I am important to someone, or that my life matters, any hardship will be bearable. Most of our struggles are centered on this quest for meaning—the search for personal significance. It is not enough to say "I think, therefore I am." Instead, we must be able to say, "I am, therefore I am valuable."

The Lord proclaims the worth of each of us in dozens of scriptures such as this one: "For the Son of man is come to save that which was lost." (Matt. 18:11.)

Most psychologists believe that a primary source of mental illness is unresolved conflict within the self. They also believe that self-acceptance is the basis for adequate health. Self-acceptance is our willingness to allow ourselves to be who we are; we do not expect that we will be who we are not. The key to self-acceptance is unconditional love of self—the ability to accept ourselves as we are.

The Apostle Paul understood and lived according to a superior interpretation of the gospel, which he had obviously internalized. This understanding deepened as he gained new knowledge, insight, and experience. "For now we see through a glass, darkly; but then face to face: now I know in part, but then shall I know even as as I am known." (1 Corinthians 13:12.)

The largest errors of humanity come not so much from ill intent as from ignorance: not knowing how to make life work better, seeing through a glass, darkly. When we learn the ways of love and are able to make our lives work better, we achieve a higher level of self. At that level we see more clearly. We want good things for ourselves and for others. We want to love and be loved. We want to do work that is significant and worthwhile. We want to be trusted and respected. We want to be happy, joyful, even abundant ... and our focus is on *being*.

Confirming Our Own Value

Having learned the importance of being, we confirm our own value with the only person to whom this really matters: ourselves. Regardless of any fears or animosity, we quietly acknowledge foes and deal with them appropriately; and when we do this, our foes are no longer our foes. With joyful knowledge we marvel that we are people and so are they. What unites us with our foes is far deeper than what divides us from them. Our fears do not terrorize or intimidate us. Our days and our nights are full of good work and good friends. Our loneliness becomes aloneness—a choice rather than a fear over which we have no control.

We are filled with hope, and at this point no philosopher, sage, psychologist, minister, or how-to book speaks for us; we speak for ourselves. Beyond the darkness and the despair is light. We are in control of ourselves. Power flows from the conviction that we alone are responsible for who we are becoming.

Our Lesser and Higher Selves

When we internalize the first way of love, acceptance, we become more deeply rooted and firmly anchored as individuals. The

fractured or lesser self—that is, the outer shell of temporary problems—is still there, but it is now seen as a friendly opposition that is
a dynamic force encouraging us to change and grow. Rather than
being channeled into destructive forces, anger is turned into quick
and powerful energy directed at a specific cause. The lesser self,
which includes tendencies toward division, contention, alienation,
and separateness, is a part of us also. The tendencies of the lesser self
are personally destructive and harmful to others. We have them in us,
but we don't have to empower them.

We all experience the battles between our lesser and our higher
selves. When I honestly assess myself, I know that I am selfish,
self-centered, and fragmented, but that I am also loving, giving, and
self-sacrificing. I need to acknowledge all of my negative and positive attributes as a part of me. I must accept the fact that both my
higher self and my lesser self will always exist. The higher self, my
spirit self, quietly and lovingly looks at the characteristics of the
divisive lesser self, takes them into control, and lovingly unifies
them. This higher self of unity and oneness is a clear voice, a voice I
long to hear, a voice that brings me home.

For example, when I spend time trying to please others inappropriately, I find that, ultimately, I just don't feel right. I finally admit
what I am doing and stop it. I sometimes want to hurt others, and I
find that when I give in to that desire I may gain power that I enjoy
temporarily. But I realize that in the long run, hurting others doesn't
work; it destroys relationships and inner self-confidence. So I
decide in advance not to be divisive the next time.

It is vital to recognize our higher selves and make a choice to be
who we really are. We want to concentrate our energies on our
greater selves, not our lesser selves.

Christ said, "I am come that they might have life, and that they
might have it more abundantly." (John 10:10.) Christ wants us to be
committed to our best selves, to live fully and abundantly, and to
develop our best talents and gifts. He does not want us to empower
the voices of deceit and despair that always send the same hurtful
messages: "You are not okay—you do not live your life right. You
aren't acceptable." These voices can be eliminated by honest admission and choice—by feeding our strengths, not our weaknesses.

Confirming and Internalizing

All deficiency motivation can be dispelled through contact with the higher self within. I am motivated by deficiency when I think I need something from outside myself to be whole. When I see the reality of abundance, all that I do flows—not out of the need to prove something, to get even, to prove my worth, or to please—but out of my inner motivation to *be*. I choose to think of the abundance of talent, beauty, and caring that is within me and to make my choices based on those attributes instead of on my deficiencies.

I recognize and acknowledge my weaknesses, not with anger or meanness, but with quiet acceptance of their reality. For example, I may realize that I have some feelings of jealousy. I don't like them and I don't want them, but I realize that they are there. It's helpful for me to acknowledge my weaknesses, to say what they are, to describe them, and then to quietly put them in their place. Identifying my weaknesses helps me discover that something better can and should be in control of my thinking and helps me get on with my life.

What I have just described is the process of internalization and confirmation. When we use it, we stand in the full sunlight of self-discovery. New words, including quietness, beauty, dignity, respect, and honor, are needed to describe the way we feel. The feelings and the reality symbolized by these words emerge from our very centers. We do what we do because these actions have meaning for us.

Internalizing the Attribute of Love

The scriptures tell us that "God is love." (1 John 4:8.) God does not simply have love or do loving acts; he *is* love. Similarly, we too can develop this type of love so that the total expression of our being is unconditional love. Having love for someone and doing something loving for that person are only the beginnings of becoming an unconditionally loving person. We move from having a desire to be accepting and nonjudgmental to actively accepting and being nonjudgmental. Taking such positive action makes it possible to internalize these characteristics so that we *are* accepting and nonjudgmental. At that point, we no longer mechanically analyze what the best response would be in a given situation. We simply respond as accepting, nonjudgmental, people in the most loving way possible. At this point we have internalized love.

A man I counselled began to experience this internalization of love as I talked with him and his wife. He was struggling with learning to listen to and accept his wife. Most of the time, he would judge her negatively, and then they would argue and blame each other. She could hardly say a word without his challenging her, and he could barely speak without her challenging him. In each counselling session for a period of several weeks I confronted them about their argumentative behavior. I asked them if they were getting what they wanted by continually challenging each other.

One day, near the end of a counselling session, the wife started talking about a time in her childhood when she was abused. Her tear-filled eyes mirrored her hurt and pain. I turned to the husband and said, "Tell me what you see in her eyes."

He started to cry. "Oh, I see all the pain."

Then they started to talk about her pain. That day was the first time in their marriage of twenty-five years that the husband had ever seen her pain as anything but a threat to him. For the first time he understood the tears and felt a momentary sense of unity and oneness with her. The skill of listening had changed from a theoretical skill he wanted to learn to an experience he could relate to, and he finally believed he could feel accepting toward his wife. Now he could say, "Ahhh! Now I know how it feels to be accepting and loving and to really listen to my wife." They began making different choices and interacting more positively as they learned to accept each other's feelings.

People will frequently get an "Ah-hah!" sensation when they realize that they have internalized a skill and have been able to understand someone else's feelings and share a bedrock experience with them.

Reverence for Life

When we develop internalization and confirmation, we come to have a reverence for life. We see that all people are valuable, even extraordinary. Nature is glorious in its variability, its color, its simplicity. We begin a love affair with nature, a relationship that will last throughout life. We value simple pleasures: we notice the subtle color transitions in the rainbow; we love to breathe deeply the early morning mountain air; we find the sunrise and the sunset to be as miraculous as an eclipse; we love to run smooth sand through our fingers; and we would rather look for stars in the sky than on a movie screen. At that point, our values lie in experiencing simple but powerful phenomena.

Internalization and confirmation cause a deep reverence for life, and nature takes hold in the heart. We value the life of the unborn and we literally internalize the old phrase "live and let live." At the fear level, we shoot a deer and capture its life. At the duty level, we take a picture of it and capture the moment for later reverie. At the love level, we quietly celebrate, in the present tense, whatever minutes we can share in the forest with the deer, having outgrown the desire to capture nature in any way.

One morning as I awakened, I thought of my own circumstances. I was staying in my friends' condominium in a place called Deer Valley in Park City, Utah. They had a sauna, a jacuzzi, and all the conveniences that modern living can afford. The place felt luxurious and in many ways wonderful. I deeply appreciated their generosity, and I spent two or three very wonderful and exciting days there writing, thinking, centering, and praying. However, these fine surroundings had little to do with what was happening inside of me. I would have been just as happy in a simple motel room or a warm, one-room cabin.

External circumstances have very little to do with what I experience and my state of being. I am influenced by the beautiful music at my command, wonderful tapes that help me relax or meditate, and recording devices that capture some of my feelings as I write my personal history. The power to center—to see snow in the trees, and to experience the warmth of sunlight, or the blowing, howling snow—is all within me; it is available to me no matter where I am. The quality of my experience depends much more on the level of my self-acceptance and my awareness of "being" than on my external circumstances.

Becoming Whole

I want to describe the "pearl-making" stage of personal development. Inside each of us during this stage, something different is happening. It happens silently, slowly, secretly. It is a searching for self.

It is not the frantic, disheveled groping for the answer to the question, "Who am I?" that occurs much earlier than this stage. It is a time of increased understanding of the self when we open our minds to deeper meaning. This stage does not involve the questions of "Who am I?" or "What am I?" anymore. Questions such as "What am I part of and what is part of me?" are asked instead, because the whole self is truly "more than the sum of its parts."

When we begin to feel whole rather than fractured we gain a calm reassurance deep inside. Will power is no longer seen as a clenched fist but as a loving discipline. Conflict and trouble are now seen as challenges and opportunities instead of burdens or taunts. Gratitude at this stage is spontaneous, not dutiful. Through this awareness, the great ship of self rises out of the troubled seas and begins to sail in clouds of peace.

Negative reasons no longer motivate us. All the old cravings, the desperate begging, and the needing are gone. The whole self has many wants and desires but no addictions. Gone is the deficiency motivation, the mental suction that takes and hoards and suffocates, all in the name of security. In its place is an urge for actualization, a releasing that gives, shares, creates. The whirlpool has become the spring. As we stand in the full sunlight of self-discovery, a quietness, a beauty, and a power emerge. This change is the result of high self-esteem and usually follows the use of the valuing skills. Remember that the Valuing System is merely a learned application of skills that comes naturally for those who are innately talented in relating to others. The Valuing System simply makes these skills easier for the rest of us to learn and use. There are other ways to learn these skills, and the people who reach the personal heights discussed here have learned them one way or another. They may never hear of the Valuing System, but they will have the rightness within from applying it instinctively.

A person who experiences wholeness has personal integrity. Inner values match actions and the real self is recognized, confirmed, valued, and accepted. Such a person values *being* more than *having* or *doing*. Henry Frederic Amiel said, "It is not what he has nor even what he does which directly expresses the work of a man, but what he is."

Having and Doing Versus the Need to Be

Children live in a state of pure being. They live totally and fully in
the moment and experience only those things relative to that
moment, with no thought of the future or the past. However, since
our society's values are centered around ownership, possessing, and
controlling—children soon adopt these values. The "having" values
lead us to the illusion that owning more or possessing more will fill
the emptiness within. When we mature, we see that the having or
owning values are severely limiting because they do not help us to
become caring, loving, genuine people. Those fortunate enough to
discover that accumulating things leads not to peace and fullness
but only to the graveyard of emptiness, change their focus.

After we find that "having" values lead only to emptiness, our next
conclusion may be that only what we *do* will provide us with meaning. We often think that if we become competent in a profession or a
trade or do other selected tasks well, we will find satisfaction and
meaning. We believe that if we become trained professionals we can
render a higher service and make our lives more meaningful. There
is a certain degree of merit in this belief and practice. As we become
competent at mothering, fathering, making a marriage work, building a strong family, being a good employee or employer, or providing a useful service in the community, our life *does* work better.
However, *doing* only partially fulfills our inner need for meaning; in
the larger view, it still misses the mark—it is but half a loaf.

After healthy individuals fulfill the need to *do*, the need to *be* may
still remain unfulfilled. The need to *be* consists of experiencing life
fully and living "in the moment." The answer is to focus *first* on
being our most authentic and loving and caring self in the present
moment. If we accomplish that, *doing* our chosen task well will follow easily and naturally.

For instance, we first need to decide that we want to be the kind
of person who creates a feeling of psychological safety for one's
self as well as others. This attitude makes it possible to draw to ourselves the conditions of life that allow us to feel accepted and valued, warts and all. We become nonjudgmental and giving, and consequently we invite that response in others. We openly and willingly
trust others even though we might get hurt. It is at this point that we
begin to experience what *being* feels like. Though we are not yet

totally nonjudgmental or giving, we are moving in the right direction: we are "in process."

What I Have Versus What I Am

Some may say that a focus on "being" instead of "having" does not realistically acknowledge the world in which we live. Of course, we can and must own, and even control at times to make life more functional. I am not saying that owning a house, a car, and a basketful of groceries does not count. These possessions do count because they fill our physical needs. But meeting these needs is only a means to a higher end—the end described throughout this book. When these physical needs have been met, the importance of higher needs emerges. (See Maslow's hierarchy of needs in his book *Motivation and Personality*.)

In the eternal sense, we do not own anything. As we move toward inevitable death, we must eventually give up all that we own and control. If we maintain a larger perspective, we can see that possessions, including our own bodies, are temporary; ownership is relative. Therefore, we have only a *stewardship* over the things we "own," even our physical bodies.

Possessions come in fixed amounts, such as a ton of coal or a roomful of furniture. But there is no fixed amount when we *are* something. We can be increasingly loving and caring throughout our lives without limitations.

To continue the analogy, when we use coal, which produces heat and waste, in the end the coal is used up. But the exercise of love or caring results in an ever increasing amount of warmth without waste. Thus *being* actually gives us more in return than *having*, since what we *are* is more permanent than what we *have*.

If we get stuck in the "having mode," the story is quite different. Even qualities such as love and caring are converted mentally, and we think of them as things we hold and possess. We may say "I have a great love for you" instead of "I love you." We don't own anything, including love. Therefore, we must be very careful not to make love a possession; we realize rather that it is an experience.

If we *are* something, such as loving and caring, then when we give that loving and caring away, we receive more in return because we become an instrument, a vessel through which we share love and caring. Sharing enriches *us* as well as the people with whom we share the gift. As we increasingly share our understanding of life, the very process of sharing with others enlarges that understanding. The more we share ourselves, the more we become. As our capacity to share expands, our capacity to receive also expands. Therefore, we become instruments through which growth and love flow.

If we cannot share our values and the meaning we find in our lives, then blockage occurs. Our ability to remain teachable and flexible diminishes, and we are no longer an instrument of fulfillment. When we share our meaning, we truly become instruments, like a clarinet or a harp, through which the music of life is played. All the love, happiness, and success we enjoy is a result of the price we have paid in time, concentration, and willingness to learn adequate principles. We allow these principles to mold our personalities until each becomes an instrument of fulfillment for ourselves and others.

When we understand clearly that having is inferior to being, we become less concerned with what we accumulate. We think less about our financial worth and more about human values. People count more than things with us. We seek possessions and ownership only as means to an end, not as ends in and of themselves.

If we place our values on owning, possessing, or controlling, an insatiable appetite is born. The more we possess, the more we think we must possess. Volume does not satisfy us; it only creates an endless, unanswerable quest. *Being* values initiate a different process. They enhance the giver and the receiver, causing each to grow, experience, and live joyfully.

The Spiritual Roots of Being

This may seem to be a discussion about something that happens to people who do not live in the real world. Not so. These stages of growth do occur and have occurred in the lives of people from St. Francis of Assisi to Abraham Lincoln and from Eleanor Roosevelt to Mother Teresa—people who are very much involved with the problems of the world. Even closer to home, you and I personally know people who have quietly, privately met their challenges and struggles with patience and meekness. These people, too, are heroes in their own spheres.

How do these people go on in the face of so much adversity? How do they not only carry on but go right on smiling? I believe they continue living happily because they feel confirmation. At the deepest level of their existence, there is an unshakable affirmation that all the harshness and unfairness of life is temporary and will, in time, be corrected and balanced. They believe that in the long run, the essential nature of all existence is good—that, indeed, the universe is friendly. After hearing a millennia of maybe's, no's, and excuses from people, they believe the final answer will be a resounding "YES!" from God, which will completely fill every corner of the universe.

Actualizers believe in the eventual spiritual balancing that comes through the Christian doctrine of grace, and they seek such confirmations from the influence and presence of the Holy Ghost in their lives. In one of his last visits with his apostles before his crucifixion, the Savior promised that though he must leave their presence, he would leave with them the gift of "the Comforter, which is the Holy Ghost." (John 14:26.)

What most of us need in this telestial world is comfort and assurance that our lives count and have meaning. The Holy Ghost is properly named the Comforter because comforting is one of his chief functions. With that comforting may also come healing or the "Balm of Gilead" spoken of in the scriptures. At times when we are feeling defeated, when the world seems to be closing in on us, we also need, in addition to comfort, courage, strength, and power to return and face the world.

We must believe in the doctrine of works as it is explained throughout the scriptures but with the understanding that good works can only take us so far. Even when we do all we can do, we are always short of the mark. Of this truth, many prophets have testified: "For by grace are ye saved through faith; and that not of yourselves: it is the gift of God." (Ephesians 2:8.)

At this point, we need to surrender ourselves to the higher power of Christ's love and grace. We need the kind of broken heart that makes us open and teachable; we need to acknowledge that we need his help. The grace of God can take us from wherever our good works have brought us and propel us into his divine love and into the highest level of self-acceptance.

Bedrock: The Fruit of Internalization and Confirmation

Bedrock means a place of openness, honesty, and trust. Bedrock is possible because of internalization and confirmation. As we grow into maturity, all our efforts, our striving, and our struggles are meant to lead us to the wonderful world of trust we call bedrock. It involves trust for and with others, but mostly trust in ourselves. Can you recall moments of personal bedrock in your own life? Such moments might be when you gaze at your sleeping child, sing a song with such meaning that you yourself are entranced, feel the power of a personal victory after you had failed many times before, meet an old friend and know immediately that it's "all still there," or remember the wonder and power when you were able to transform a setting of dangerous conflict into one of real trust. A special feeling comes at such times—times when you might say to yourself, "It doesn't get any better than this." This feeling of oneness with others and trust in ourselves is the real world we long for, and it is a world we can create.

Many of our deepest bedrocks are not created in our relationships with others; they are created within ourselves as we experience our larger spiritual power. Most of our key moments in life occur when we spend quiet time alone. At this level of bedrock, our relationships are not crucial to our existence. Instead, deepening and strengthening our individual spirit is paramount.

To achieve a personal bedrock, we need to ask ourselves the following questions:

- Do I feel safe with me? Is it okay that I have many imperfections?

- Can I look at my behaviors, thoughts, and feelings objectively?

- When I answer these questions negatively, can I still believe that I am worthwhile and truly wonderful?

- Can I ask questions about my own meaning as I discover and rediscover what I want?

- Can I answer myself honestly, knowing that a price tag comes with my decision?

- Do I have the desire to search almost constantly for the meaning of my life, realizing that during much of my life, I must maintain a balance between searching and finding?

- Can I accept that from each discovery, a new need for searching begins? That out of each new search comes another discovery? That I clearly alternate back and forth between the process of *becoming* and the process of *being*?

• Can I continue to affirm my own worth, to confirm my own experience, and to validate the very purpose of my existence?

The Path That Leads to Bedrock

I believe and have observed it to be true that in order to experience and internalize bedrock we are likely to follow a very identifiable path:

1. *We experience significant hardship or trouble*—sometimes over a long period of time. We learn to handle this trouble well; as a result of it, we grow in power and capacity. For the Lord sends the rain upon "the just and the unjust" and has declared: "My people must be tried in all things."

Adversity does not make us bitter, cynical, or hostile. It makes us accepting, forgiving, and quietly strong: "We are troubled on every side, yet not distressed; we are perplexed, but not in despair; Persecuted, but not forsaken; cast down, but not destroyed." (2 Corinthians 4:8-9.)

2. *Through experience with success and failure, we learn how to turn failure into success.* We come to define success in a totally new way, rarely defining success in terms of what we own, possess, or control, nor in terms of what we do. Success to us is what we are. We experience fully what each day has to offer and our relationships are full and exciting.

3. *We learn to live fully in the here and now, even in day-to-day "compartments."* For example, we compartmentalize our worries by leaving business troubles at the office. We also accept the reality that we cannot change the past. We enjoy each moment as it is without thrusting ourselves into the future or worrying about the past.

4. *We experience all three levels of being.* We have experienced the trauma, frustrations, and anger of the fear/anxiety level of living, and although we have willingly and finally left that world behind, we remember it and have empathy for those who are still living there.

We later chose and accepted a duty/justice existence. We became entwined and tangled in the rewards and punishment system of this society. While we were at this level, we felt there was something more to life, so we chose to move in an upward direction. We kept changing because half a loaf was not enough. We decided we wanted all life had to offer—the whole thing.

We reach the love/trust level by choosing in realistic ways to be trusting and to build trust with others. We learn to find bedrock, how to act on that bedrock, and how to build relationships that have depth and power. We know how to be honest with ourselves, how to center, how to find our own power, how to choose strengthening behaviors. Indeed, we know how to be strong enough to be loving.

5. *Each of us makes the choice to truly be his own person and choose his own road.* "I can't be right for somebody else if I'm not right for me" (from "I Gotta Be Me," a song by Walter Marks). Our self-esteem is high and we almost always choose a life task or a life's work that is important to us. At this level we are not concerned with proving anything to anyone else; we haven't practiced deficiency motivation for a long time. We choose important, satisfying work, and we do it with dedication and commitment.

How Bedrock Affects Our Lives

When we experience and internalize bedrock, many aspects of life change. For example, at the fear/anxiety level, we have difficulty internalizing will power. (We say, "I *must* do this," as though something "out there" is controlling us.) However, when achieving the love/trust level, we feel calmer and more relaxed, but much stronger, and say, "I choose to do this for my own long-term strength." When we achieve this level, we no longer challenge ourselves to avoid conflict. When conflict arises, we simply remind ourselves that we can effectively solve the conflicts and then move ahead to find ways to do so. We seek alternatives not out of anger but out of quiet self-control. We don't think about *creating* a safe place for our family—we simply *are* a safe place for them. When we perceive that someone is playing games, we intuitively confront that person. We ask him or her to stop playing games in a way that doesn't result in a win/lose situation. We identify the game for what it is and identify its harmful consequence. We don't take a small problem and blow it out of proportion. We make sure that what is important in our lives comes first.

Quickly, easily, and without force, we quietly quit choosing up sides and stop blaming others for our problems. More importantly, when we know that we're off target, the inner sense of rightness we have developed is so strong that we quickly realize that there is a problem. We stop, admit that we have acted inappropriately, and then take better actions. Our gyroscope is fully working and highly reliable.

Let me show you how that principle has worked in my life. One day I belittled one of my sons in front of his friends for not doing his chores. I first read the embarrassment on his face, and then I saw it on his friends' faces as well.

When I realized what I was doing, I stopped talking for a minute and then said, "I have made a big mistake and I don't want to make it worse. I didn't intend to have a battle with you and certainly not in front of your friends. I can see how embarrassed you are. Can we talk privately for just a minute and see if we can make this better?"

Relief filled my son's eyes and then his friends' faces.

We went in the other room and he said, "You didn't give me a chance to say what I wanted to say."

I replied, "That's true. So let's talk now and I will listen. Let's make an agreement that we won't leave until we both feel okay." The problem was quickly resolved. My son and I hugged each other and he went back to his friends.

Through this experience, I learned that relationships count more than issues and that trust counts more than being right.

Once the skills of trusting, loving, accepting, and not judging become automatic through repeated usage, the confirmation process takes over. As we *internalize* these skills, they are confirmed within us (by confirmed, I mean habitual and unlikely to change). Our nervous system has been reprogrammed to be our ally. This way of love, along with all the others, express what reality is for me. The ways of love follow the ways of truth. They are growth-producing, expanding, and unifying; they help us create win/win relationships. This belief system can help us grow and help others begin to use the characteristics of the higher self.

Bedrock in Relationships

Truly *being*, in the framework of relationships, is to experience the bedrock of trust. When we reach the bedrock of trust, we have a rich experience that involves feeling accepted by another person. We drop our defenses and can be honest and open. We feel no need to argue. We trust the other person. It does not matter that we have each made mistakes. We don't need to defend ourselves or pretend. The bedrock is like an end point, an "arrived at," wonderful place. It is not *processing*, not *becoming*, but *being* there.

The Skill of Listening

The first step in this process of becoming a truly loving person and achieving bedrock in relationships is to try to listen to others' feelings. At first, we may be mechanical and awkward in our efforts. However, because of our increased efforts to listen, others will view us as safer, more sensitive, and more caring than we were before. We learn that becoming nonjudgmental and caring opens doors that have long been closed. As we experience the benefits of more open relationships, we are encouraged to do *more* listening and be *more* accepting. Therefore, as we take a skill "out there" and start using it, the skill becomes more and more a part of us. In fully developing a trait, such as being a good listener, all traces of awkwardness eventually disappear. As we completely internalize the skill of listening, we are no longer "trying to listen to others"—we simply *are* good listeners. We no longer guess whether the time to create safe and trusting conditions is right; we just consistently act. We don't *have* skills—we *are* skilled.

Using Valuing Questions

In the following scenario, valuing questions help a father and son trust each other enough to stop blaming each other and start working on their relationship. In the end they reach bedrock and finally accept the fact that relationships count more than issues. By using a combination of bribes and threats, this father succeeded in getting his son to come with him to a counselling session with me. The son showed his obvious displeasure with the setting by slouching in his chair and pulling his cowboy hat down over his eyes. Then the father began a litany of complaints about the son such as, "He takes drugs and drinks. He won't do what he's told and he is disrespectful." At these remarks, the son withdrew even more. So I began asking the father some valuing questions.

"It's obvious your relationship with your son is not working. Is that okay with you?"

"No, it's not okay."

"When you get on your son's case about his bad behavior, how does he respond?"

"He gets worse and he becomes more arrogant and rebellious, and then he withdraws."

"Is it true then that what you are doing isn't working?"

"Yes, but can't you see how he's hurting me and hurting the family?"

"If we agree that you are right and he is wrong about all this, has it helped or hurt your relationship with him?"

"Hurt, I guess."

"Is that what you want?"

"No."

"What do you want with your son?"

"A better relationship. I want him to treat our family better."

"If we can't achieve that by finding out who is wrong and who is right, do you think we could achieve it by building trust?"

"I don't know how."

"Would you like to learn how?"

"Yes."

"Can you tell your son how you feel about these things?"

The father sat and thought for a few moments, then turned to his son and told him that he was very sorry that their relationship wasn't working out better. He also told his son that he was afraid of losing him and that he loved him greatly. The son was surprised and emotionally touched.

By this time, as you can imagine, the son was taking a more positive interest and my conversation with the son went like this:

"You seem to know how to control your father—to make him uncomfortable and unhappy?"

"No—I feel like he's trying to control me. He's always telling me what to do."

"When he tells you what to do, what do you do?"

"Usually just the opposite."

"Then what happens?"

"He jumps on my case and blames me more."

"So what you do doesn't help either?"

"Yes, I guess."

"What kind of things do you do that weaken your relationship with your family?"

"I admit I'm hard to live with. I just want out."

"Aside from your family, do you also have problems with other relationships?"

"I guess so."

"So, could it be to your advantage to learn better ways of dealing with conflict?"

"Yes."

"Can you tell your father this?"

[After a long silence (four to five minutes)]:"Dad, I know I've been hard to live with. I just feel bad all the time. I don't know what to do."

At this point both father and son reached a new level of trust, for they quit blaming each other and they both stated that they wanted to work together. After discovering key concepts (that what they were doing wasn't working and neither of them was getting what they wanted), they could break the cycle of hostility by learning some communication skills, such as accepting and leveling.

When we reach bedrock, we really trust ourselves and others. At the bedrock level we stop manipulating others and playing games. Then we learn what it feels like to truly experience another person without defenses, shame, or pretense. Bedrock brings a simplicity, love, and knowledge that our relationship is going to work. Where does this deep self-trust, even reverence, come from?

Creating Equal Relationships

Once we have learned how to obtain a feeling of trust or bedrock in our relationships and know what it tastes like, we develop a hunger for it. Our ordinary experiences pale in comparison. We develop a hunger and a thirst to build that trust again. However, this process cannot be forced. It comes through acceptance, quietness, and centering. It comes from quieting the outer noise and listening to the inner peace. Bedrock is the result of a commitment to stop ourselves from acting out of anger and choosing instead to act according to positive feelings. We avoid fighting, running, and ignoring others because we know that taking negative action does not lead to bedrock and trust; it leads to further alienation and the inability to experience both ourselves and other people the way we truly want and need to.

An equal relationship requires deep respect both for oneself and for the other person in the relationship. In a truly equal relationship, put-downs and superior and inferior positions are unacceptable. Equality has much to do with recognition and acceptance of the value of every person, including ourselves.

The more we experience bedrock in our relationships, the more we will be capable of creating equal relationships. As we increase our ability in this area, we will find that we can create conditions that bring about bedrock more frequently. In general, we will come to feel very comfortable in bedrock situations with friends, family, and coworkers. Bedrock will occur more often and it will remain longer. We will experienced it with peace and quietness. Life itself will become more pleasant and the people we are with will become more friendly. After we develop a feeling of trust and bedrock, we miss it greatly if we do not have it. When we do have it, we have the feeling of "coming home," of being in tune with our essential self and with others.

Uncovering and Accepting the Light Within

To his disciples who were rebuking crowds of followers asking for their children to be blessed, Jesus said, "Suffer little children to come unto me, and forbid them not: for of such is the kingdom of God." (Luke 18:16.) In other words, Christ wants us to re-find our innocence. When we know that each of us is born with the light of Christ (John 1:9), this truth can teach us that deep in every human being is something very pure, full of light and hope. Yet we tend to mask this light within behind a thousand faces while we live in this telestial world.

A modern religious leader described the Lord's way of removing our false identities in the following passage: "The Lord works from the inside out. The world works from the outside in. The world would take people out of the slums. Christ takes the slums out of people, and they take themselves out of the slums. The world would mold men by changing their environment. The world would shape human behavior, but Christ can change human nature."

As we grow into love/trust people, we develop the courage to remove the masks to reveal who we truly are. We have grown to be afraid of ourselves, but we need not be, because the wellspring of truth lies deep in each of us.

One reason a contrite spirit is so important is because such humility reveals our true character: that we are prone to mistakes and errors. When we are willing to correct errors by being teachable and surrendering to spiritual experiences, we learn that we are part of something big, wondrous, and whole, and that the universe is part of us. The more deeply we discover our own natures, both our weaknesses and our strengths, the more our inner light emerges, leading us to the freedom and strength to some day see the face of God.

Why then, if this light is so deep within us, are there so many scriptures instructing us to "ask and ye shall receive"? It is because our need to ask and acknowledge our limits is deeply connected to God's willingness to be there for us and meet our needs as no human being can. I have found that in my darkest discouragement, no human being can reach me deeply enough to turn that discouragement around. At these times, my mind must be surrendered to something larger, something higher—to my creator, to my God.

Your personal search for meaning will be fruitless as long as you seek for your "holy grail" to be fulfilled through some source outside yourself. You will cheat yourself of it as long as your self-acceptance is based on the approval of others, accomplishment or possessions.

The Peace Found Within

According to the scriptures, Solomon built a temple to allow the Israelites to better worship God. There were three separate areas in the temple: the outer courtyard, the Holy Place, and the Holy of Holies. This last room could be entered only after the individual went through the two outer areas. It was a profoundly sacred place only the prophet could enter to converse with God. The process of finding the true self is analogous to the process required for one to enter the Holy of Holies. We will find our true selves within our own Holy of Holies only after we have left behind our maze of negative ideas, labels, and approval-seeking behavior.

The essay "Desiderata" describes how we can experience peace, power, and balance:

> Go placidly amid the noise and haste and remember what peace there may be in silence. As far as possible without surrender, be on good terms with all persons. Speak your truth quietly and clearly; and listen to others, even the dull and the ignorant; they too have their story. Avoid loud and aggressive persons, they are vexations to the spirit. If you compare yourself with others you may become vain and bitter for always there will be greater and lesser persons than yourself. Enjoy your achievements as well as your plans. Keep interested in your own career, however humble; it is a real possession in the changing fortunes of time. Exercise caution in your business affairs; for the world is full of trickery. But let not this blind you to the virtue there is; many persons strive for high ideals and everywhere life is full of heroism. Be yourself. Especially, do not feign affection. Neither be cynical about love, for in the face of all aridity and disenchantment, it is perennial as grass. Take kindly the counsel of the years, gracefully surrendering the things of youth. Nurture strength of spirit to shield you in sudden misfortune. But do not distress yourself with imaginings. Many fears are born of fatigue and loneliness. Beyond a wholesome discipline, be gentle with yourself. You are a child of the universe no less than the trees and the stars; you have a right to be here. And whether or not it is clear to you, no doubt the universe is unfolding as it should. Therefore, be at peace with God, whatever you conceive Him to be, and whatever your labors and aspirations, in the noisy confusion of life, keep peace with your soul. With all its sham and drudgery and broken dreams, it is still a beautiful world. Be careful. Strive to be happy. (Max Ehrman.)

Thus, as we internalize the process of confirming our own value, we can reach deep levels of bedrock within. We learn to manage our lesser and higher selves and rejoice in our wholeness and reverence for all of life. As we do this we will receive a quiet assurance that through us some of the goodwill of the world will spread. As we are willing to continue to grow and share, much of the goodness that now resides in others can also become ours.

I invite you to let yourself *be*. Open your heart and let the light of your true self shine out. Accept your real self and its true nature as being of innate and infinite value. You have nothing to prove; there are no conditions. You have met the enemy. He is not you but your fear of yourself. End your inner war with a flood of warm and welcoming tears, a catharsis of spiritual amnesty. You are already whole. Give yourself the only gift that really matters—acceptance. Celebrate your being. The cabin is warm and waiting. Come home.

THE FOURTH WAY OF LOVE: SHARED MEANING THROUGH A NEW KIND OF GIFT-GIVING

The fourth way of love is this: *Living with an abundance of peace, awareness, and joy, we become whole. Since we have no need to count costs or get credit, we desire to share that joy and its meaning with others. Our desire is to share our center, our most intrinsic meaning, "the pearl" within us.*

Introduction

The finest gift we can give to anyone is the gift of genuine caring. When we care what happens to another person and sincerely value him or her, a bond is forged between us and the other person that goes beyond technique.

When the joy of personal meaning is so intense that we can't hold it in, our spirits seem to have no walls; we want to share ourselves. As I share my meaning with you and you accept and value it, we are both enhanced. When you open up to me, you feel fulfilled, and I am made better by your gift and by the very act of sharing. When I appreciate you, you are made richer still.

Many scriptures refer to giving and receiving, including the following:

"Ask, and it shall be given you." (Luke 11:9.)

"Freely ye have received, freely give." (Matthew 10:8.)

"Come unto me, all ye that labour and are heavy laden, and I will give you rest." (Matthew 11:28.)

"For unto everyone that hath shall be given." (Matthew 25:29.)

Kahil Gibran says, "You give but little when you give of your possessions. It is when you give of yourself that you truly give." Our greatest value, he says, lies in our commitment to a relationship, and in our knowledge, wisdom, experience, and insight. Nothing that we own is close to being of the same value as that which we are. Meaningful gifts are always gifts of self.

Some gifts of meaning may have little practical use—such as the primitive crayon drawing of "a house with people in it" that your kindergartner proudly brings home for you to display on the refrigerator door; the rusted old brooch your grandmother gives you with trembling hands; the moving passage from your favorite poem, book, film, or song that you tearfully share; the secret dream of your heart that you reveal to me softly; and the tears of joy that I, without shame, allow to flow in your presence.

Gifts of meaning are given when we deliberately and joyously conceive a new life, when an immigrant carefully teaches the old culture to his children to preserve a sense of identity with the past, when your teacher calls you aside to tell you that your comments add so much to the class, when you write a once-in-a-lifetime letter of appreciation to your father. Material gifts or those with entertainment value normally wear out with time or become dated and lose their worth, but gifts of meaning become more precious as the years go by. When we give meaning to the moments and the mementos of our lives, we create real treasures—treasures that may be passed on to our posterity as a joyous heritage of love.

Giving Strengthening Gifts

In our relationships, gifts that strengthen others may not be easy to give; we must stretch toward the love/trust life in order to be able to give them. This kind of giving requires more effort than we've ever expended before—not hand-clenched, teeth-gritting effort, but a long-suffering, patient, unselfish effort that flows from our deepest commitments. This effort is fueled by the quiet strength of knowing the truth and committing to live true principles.

Giving that is motivated by love requires great strength. It does not ask for temporary solutions or simplistic and unrealistic answers. It asks difficult questions that require both discipline and risk in relationships. Unless the theory of love becomes a part of our everyday lives, it will forever remain only a theory.

To determine whether our gifts of love are real and strengthening, we must ask ourselves several pointed questions evaluating others' and our own increased or decreased capacity to effectively cope with the world and its problems:

1. As a result of our interaction, have I increased the other person's capacity to go back and deal more effectively with his task?
2. Have we mutually improved our capacity to solve life's problems?
3. Do we enhance and strengthen each other?
4. Is our relationship strengthening our capacity to live life with more joy and to live abundantly?

When giving from a position of love/trust we can always answer these questions with a resounding "Yes!"

Examples of strengthening gifts include the following:

1. Listening to and accepting another person unconditionally. It is important that when we're with another, we are completely *with* him. (If I listen to you only mechanically or halfheartedly, you will always know. However, if I listen with my heart and show that I care for you, any techniques I may use will be peripheral to that caring.) The more we care in a loving relationship, the stronger that relationship will be.
2. Attempting to stop hostility in a constructive way so that both people win.
3. Attempting, through the use of mild confrontation, to stop game-playing and manipulating so that each person is encouraged to be open and honest with the other.
4. Asking valuing questions to change the focus from short-term decisions with quick payoffs to long-term decisions that are likely to get us what we really want.

The best gift for those who are disappointed or who feel they have failed may be to give them the strength of simple acceptance. At other times, the best gift may be empathy. Empathy involves listening to understand and not to judge; and as we practice empathy, others will open up their lives to us.

Avoiding Illusions

In contrast, excessive sympathy, like pity, is weakening. Sympathy may mean that we give pity or pass moral judgments, characterizing actions as good or bad, or people as kind or unkind. Whereas empathy is a gift of real love that leads to acceptance and safety, sympathy only reinforces cycles of weakening behavior.

The problem we have with giving is that we get trapped into practicing counterfeits or illusions of love. These illusions may persuade us into thinking that we are loving someone when we are only temporarily helping that person to feel better. A good example is the mother who thinks she is being loving by waiting on her children; instead of teaching them, she is depriving them of learning the skills of self-care.

Many people have good intentions, but they weaken friends and family with advice, sympathy, or nifty plans. They impose their own solutions, pat others on the back, assure them that everything will be all right, and then go about their business, often unaware that the person they wanted to help remains weak and dependent and lacks self-reliance. We cannot strengthen others unless we help them find their own strength and allow them to choose their own solutions. The real gift lies in teaching others how to fish rather than feeding them from our catch.

Can a person giving real gifts and demonstrating real love remain compassionate while nevertheless refusing to buy into the weakening illusions of love? Yes, because real love becomes stronger as the powerful bricks and mortar of self-esteem are put into place. This real love gives the individual a firm, unshakable foundation on which to stand in the aftermath of his trials.

Strengthening Conversation

My son, Dr. Roger K. Allen, clearly understood this principle when he went to the hospital to visit a woman who had her leg amputated from the knee down due to a serious case of diabetes. Here is his story in his own words.

> The woman was feeling quite depressed and cynical. She complained that her life would never be the same. Concerned, her husband tried desperately to reassure her that everything would be okay, but his efforts were futile. The more he tried to cheer her up, the more depressed she became.
>
> After witnessing this interaction between the husband and wife for a few minutes, I decided to risk talking plainly to the woman in the

hopes I might help her. I began by using empathy, telling her that I could appreciate that losing her leg was physically and emotionally painful. She cried, and replied, "My whole world seems turned upside down."

With a desire to strengthen her, I said, "The reality is you've lost your leg and nothing can be done to bring it back. It would be easy now to leave the hospital feeling cynical, defeated, and depressed. Are you willing to live that way?"

After a pause she said, "You don't realize how I feel and everything I've been through."

"No," I said, "I don't. I have never experienced what you are experiencing and I certainly hope I will never have to. But are you willing to go home and be as depressed and unhappy as you are right now? Many people probably are willing to do so after going through an experience like yours."

"Well, I never really thought about it like that."

"There are a lot of payoffs you can get by being unhappy," I said.

"What do you mean?"

"Little rewards, little benefits you can get. Could we talk about some of them?"

She was having trouble coming up with any, so I said, "You would get sympathy. Sympathy could be a great substitute for love."

"I guess that's true."

"Can you think of any others?"

"Well, it would be safe. I wouldn't have to take any risks."

"That's another good payoff."

"I could probably get my husband and maybe my children to do things for me."

"Right. What else?"

We identified self-pity as another payoff and also as a substitute for love. When she felt that no one else would be there, feeling sorry for herself would be a way of indulging herself.

We concluded that she could be "right" or justified in feeling that the members of her family had let her down, that people didn't really care about her, or that God had abandoned her in some way.

After we identified four or five payoffs, I said, "Not only are there payoffs that we get out of being unhappy, but there are also some pretty tough prices to pay in order to be happy. Can you think of some of those?"

She thought for a moment. "I'd need to get used to this leg. I'd need to learn to walk using an artificial leg and to get used to the pain and discomfort of it. I'd also need to get used to going out in public and letting other people see me without being embarrassed about my leg."

She realized that she would have to stop complaining and seeking sympathy from other people, that she would have to take responsibility for her own happiness, and that there were some risks that she would need to take in order to again be involved in some of the activities of the past. After she had identified some of the prices, I asked her if she thought it would be worth it—giving up the payoffs and paying the prices to live a normal life. She said that it would.

As we concluded the conversation, I noticed a genuine change in the woman, in her attitude, and even in her countenance. She moved from seeing her handicap as a limitation and feeling cynical and depressed to recognizing that she had choices about it. She began to realize that she could live a normal and productive life. (Allen, Dr. Roger K. and Hardman, Dr. Randy K., from *Making Things Happen*, a tape set produced by the Human Development Institute.)

Some people, hospital patients among them, may feel that pity is a close enough substitute to love; but pity is a false illusion of love. One who is sick may feel more valued as a person because people come to visit. But the gift of real love is the gift of strength. When I truly love, I don't so much give of my strength to you; rather, I help you to recognize your own strength.

Giving That Lasts a Lifetime

A Chinese proverb states if you "give a man a fish . . . you feed him for a day. Teach a man to fish and you feed him for a lifetime." In other words, it takes less effort to give a man a fish than to teach him to fish, and his immediate gratitude may seem very rewarding. But if I start giving him a fish daily, then every day he will be dependent on me for another fish. After a few days, he may even demand his daily fish. However, if I take the time and put forth the effort to teach him to fish, I strengthen him so that he grows in his capacity, confidence, and ability. Soon, he no longer needs my direction, and he discovers that he is able to care for himself.

Let's look at an example in the real world. Assume that I give a thousand dollars to someone who is destitute and in need. I may have helped the person temporarily, but if he hasn't developed the capacity to solve his financial problems, received training for a job, learned better job interviewing skills, or written a better resume, in a month he will just need more money. I will have created a weakening cycle of dependency. If I give him, instead, encouragement that strengthens his self-confidence, and he relies on himself to solve the problem, then I have given the greater gift. As I share my love and my meaning, I am teaching others to "fish."

Our society values fish-giving; it is generous with money and commodities. Sometimes—as in the case of a natural disaster— money, food, or clothing may be the most appropriate gift. But for individuals in everyday circumstances, such gifts can be terribly weakening.

The Gift of Loving Confrontation

Sometimes our gift of real love is best shared when we confront another person who is harming a relationship, although using confrontation only works when we are committed to a win/win outcome. When we *lovingly* confront others, we do not have the desire to put them down, to impose our ideas of how to do something, or to manipulate them in any way. Neither will we allow someone else to "con" or manipulate us, because we will recognize that as equally unloving behavior.

Let me give you an example of using confrontation as a powerful tool of love.

When I was a bishop (a position of leadership in my church), a young man in my ward came to me asking for financial help. His hair was long and not clean, his clothes dirty, his beard unkempt, and his attitude hostile. He slouched in his chair and complained that no one would give him a job. His face and voice were full of anger.

Either I could have chosen to sympathize with this young man, since I wanted to be his friend, or I could have condemned him. Instead of choosing either of these attitudes, I looked him straight in the eye and said,

"I wouldn't hire you either."

"I knew it! You're just like the rest of those jerks," he said defiantly.

"Why do you think I wouldn't hire you?"

"You don't like my hair—you probably hate my clothes."

"Do you really want a job? You don't act like you really want one to me. Maybe you want people to turn you down," I said.

"I do want a job!" he said emphatically.

"What do you think you could do to get a job?"

"Well, I'd have to dress up, maybe get a haircut."

"Would that help?"

"Sure."

"What about your attitude? I'm more concerned with that than the way you look. Will your hostility help you get a job?"

"Probably not."

"Okay, I want you to practice with me. Pretend I'm the employer, and you are coming to me for work. What are you going to say?"

We rehearsed the phrases he would use to convince a prospective boss that he would be good for the company. His skills at being interviewed improved greatly. We used a tape recorder so he could recognize and change his angry voice and his defiant attitude. I gave him feedback such as, "That sounded better, but could you do it still better?" We practiced for about forty-five minutes.

Less than two days later, he came to me wearing a suit, his face clean shaven and his hair washed and cut. He had gotten a job and he was delighted.

Using confrontation was the most loving way I could deal with this young man. It helped him make his own decisions, which were based on strengthening rather than weakening choices. My gift to him was to help him face the realities of looking for a job, and his gift to me was to listen and to apply what I taught him. I didn't make the rules of the marketplace, but my honest confrontation helped this young man see the value of making changes in order to conform to those rules and consequently get a job. I taught him "how to fish."

Helping Others Share the Gift of Love

One day I was giving a friend and her children a ride home. She had just given an inspiring address on self-esteem to a large group of adults, and both of us were feeling quite wonderful about it.

Her young sons, ages six and twelve, began bickering over a toy in the back seat. She ignored their misbehavior as long as she could, but the argument turned into a fight and she finally shouted at the older boy: "Leave him alone, you big bully!" An embarrassed silence settled over the car until we reached her home.

The boys went inside alone and their mother turned to me with tears in her eyes and said, "I did it wrong, didn't I?"

This was an important moment for me. Would I strengthen her or weaken her by my response? I answered that there were several different ways she could have responded to her sons, and I showed her the commitment process and how it works. We discussed how she could strengthen her sons instead of weakening them. She thought carefully and resolved to make a better choice the next time.

Later, she sat down with her older son and talked to him about his relationship with his younger brother. She acknowledged that she had judged him unfairly, and they talked about how they both could make better choices. She allowed him to decide what he wanted from their relationship and helped him to be responsible for himself and for solving his own problems.

She next followed the same pattern with her younger son. Over time, this practice dramatically changed the behavior of her family. As her children learned what they needed to change to get the results they wanted—that is, better relationships with each other—they became more responsible for their own actions.

Helping people take responsibility for themselves is a far more loving practice than taking sides in an argument. Learning to take responsibility gives any person more capacity to deal effectively with conflict.

New Perspectives on Giving

Giving and Receiving—A Two-Way Street

Any time you give a gift and it is received, the receiver is enhanced. In turn, in this enhanced and wiser state, the receiver can become the giver. Armed with this new, magnified meaning, the receiver then gives back to the giver his own gift, an act that enhances the original giver. The giver and the receiver regularly switch roles. In this mutual sharing of gifts, the actual act of love unfolds. Do not wait for someone else to start the process, although at times others may give first. Give your gift joyously, exuberantly, tenderly, and appropriately. The chart on the next page will help you visualize the process.

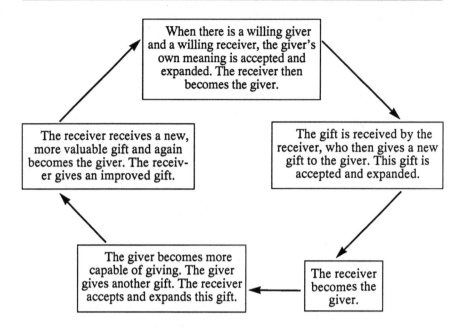

Here's how the process works: Let's assume I have recently noticed that a friend of mine has been despondent, angry, and resentful—usually clear signals that all is not right with her world. As part of my meaning, I recognize that I value her and respect her as a person. I want my relationship with her not only to continue but to be enlarged and enhanced. The gift I give her may well unfold like this:

"Jan, I would like to talk for a few minutes if you have some time today."

She receives my gift by saying, "Okay, I would like to do that. I have been wanting to talk with you for some time."

We have mutually exchanged a gift. I risked a little to approach her, and she responded by saying she valued me and my time. Later, when we talk, I say, "Looks like things have been a little bit tough lately. I've noticed that you have been somewhat angry."

She may at first reject my words and say, "No, things are fine for me. I am okay. Don't worry about me." Or she may say she's tried talking about it and it doesn't help, so it's no use talking. But if I sense that something is really wrong, I will simply remain quiet to show that I am accepting and caring.

Since she really wants to talk, my patience results in her opening up: "Yes, things are not really going very well for me. I am having troubles on this job." She might then express anger, frustration, and a belief that her life is not working very well.

The gift that this friend is giving me is the gift of trust and confidence. She is thanking me for being sensitive. So while, in the beginning, I was giving the gift by being willing to listen, now she is giving me a reciprocal gift. She has become willing to risk some of herself; she allows me to see some of her pain and frustration.

As I listen and accept her pain, and then appropriately reflect her feelings, I accept where she is. She again discloses more and more of her fears, and more and more of her anger, frustration, and loneliness. As we exchange worthwhile gifts, we now achieve that wonderful state of trust—bedrock. Here we trust each other, we value each other. We both feel safe, we don't need to weigh words or to be careful in what we say. We appreciate each other more than we did before, and we value our friendship more. We have been mutually benefitted.

As I help her identify and clarify what she wants (I again offer the gift of my understanding), this trust helps her to be clear about what she truly wants, what she needs to do to make her life work better, what harmful attitudes or cop-outs she has developed, and what the results of this behavior are. So she looks at the commitments she is willing to make in order to win back control of her life. As her course becomes clear through the process of commitment, she solves her problems with more clarity, vision, and skill than she ever has before. She gives me valuable feedback as she helps me know what part of my effort in her behalf is helpful and what is not. Thus, she gives me evidence that my time, concern, and life are worth something.

So my friend and I, in a series of gift exchanges, complete the cycle of gift-giving. Both of us are enhanced and improved in our capacity. Feeling more confident and successful through this problem solving process, we develop a greater confidence in each other as well as in ourselves. We are reassured that if this process works in this relationship, it can work elsewhere. Relationships that have been rigid or frozen can be thawed through this process. The daily conflicts, which have ended badly so often, need not defeat us any more. The wellsprings of hope begin again to work their remarkable power in this literally life-giving exchange.

The fourth way of love—increased meaning through gift-giving— is such an integral part of our lives on the love/trust level that it is impossible to imagine living without giving or without joyfully receiving. It is as natural as breathing, as necessary as eating, and on a spiritual level, as soon as we taste of the living waters, we immediately must share.

Risking and Sharing Wisely

You might say, "But I can't share with everyone!" You are right. Sharing must be done appropriately. We need to be sensitive to those who will accept our gifts, and we must realize that finding someone with whom to share is a skill. When we share with someone, we take a risk that the person will break the confidence that we have created and destroy the trust and gift that were given. Yes, sharing is a risk. But we cannot create the life we want by staying in a comfortable, no-risk posture. If we want to live a rich life, we must be on the higher end of the risking continuum. If we take no risks, then circumstances take over and control us and we give up control of all we do. If we take more risks, we will be hurt more, but we will also have closer friendships and be more capable of creating a full life.

Of course, we cannot share equally with everyone. Sometimes we must let go of a relationship that has involved sharing because trust has broken down, personalities are conflicting, or other factors have led to an inability to share appropriately. But suppose you were wounded in a sharing friendship and you are tempted to close down and to withdraw from the sharing process entirely. Closing down is not only a disservice to others, it stops the process of giving within you. It sets up blocks and stops growth. To deny yourself the opportunity to share is to dam the full development of your own meaning.

You may have a relationship that you value, but your conversation seems stuck on superficial and meaningless trivia. You would be offering a gift of love to stop the triviality and speak of what matters. Or if a friend gives you double messages, confusing you and being unclear about what he or she wants, the best gift of meaning in this situation is to stop such a game. Speaking honestly and directly—not withholding what you really think or what you really are—establishes genuine value and respect between the two of you.

Only as your meaning is appropriately shared is it brought into full flower. Mutual sharing of meaning is a pure act of love. At Robert Louis Stevenson's funeral, his friends carried the coffin to the place of interment on a mountaintop. A stranger appeared at the funeral, to which only close friends had been invited. This man, a Scotsman, explained that some years previously, Stevenson had met him on the road on a critical day. The Scotsman had been contemplating suicide. Stevenson shared with the Scotsman his belief in the value of life and persuaded the man not to take his own life. This act of sharing so deeply impressed the Scotsman that he attended Stevenson's funeral to pay homage to him and to reverently remember the glorious gift the writer had given him.

The gifts of meaning are best given quietly, without fanfare, and with no thought of reward. Sometimes my greatest gift may be to share an insight—a confirmation of knowledge that increases understanding. When we share insights, we open ourselves to the possibility of a powerful, beautiful experience. And when we learn to give unconditionally, we begin a cycle of successful sharing that can have unlimited benefits.

Sharing requires risk because our gift may be rejected and we may feel pain. But if we do not share, we take the greater risk. By refusing to take risks, by withdrawing and becoming spectators to the world, our lives become narrow, shallow, and superficial. Eventually, we become half-alive, then only twenty-five percent, then only ten percent. Those who do not reverse this process eventually become emotionally, psychologically, and spiritually dead. Because they refuse to take risks, a closing-down process occurs. This closing down is the ultimate risk, for it leads to damage to the real self and finally to emotional death. To live we must risk. To live we must share.

Motivational and Mutual Sharing

The process of gift-giving is diminished, even negated, if my motive is to get credit for the gift, to be recognized, to have my ego fed, to assuage my pride, or to obtain a superior position. If I am the "teacher" and know too much and my friend is the "pupil" who knows too little, or if I am the "big" one and she is the "little" one, hurtful imbalances are created. If gaining superiority is my motivation for gift-giving, this need to feel "better" or more "right" actually stops or impedes the process. Respect for equality is the key.

A subtle but powerful distinction exists between teaching and sharing. While some people are obviously more trained or knowledgeable than others on certain subjects (teachers, for instance, need to know more than their students), the difference is in the attitude of respect that the more knowledgeable or powerful person has for the person who knows less or who has less power. Examples of this relationship are the doctor's attitude toward the patient, the professor's attitude toward the student, and the employer's attitude toward the employee.

The difference, then, between teaching and sharing is found in *respect* rather than knowledge, social position, or the power to hire and fire. Many people give lip service to this notion, but it is rarely practiced, hence division and alienation are created. Acceptance is often overlooked by those who would be "teachers" in personal relationships. This unequal, "big me/little you" relationship subtly undermines the ability of those involved to communicate love to each other. Mutual sharing is imperative if any real help is to be given. Therefore, we must try to see whether safe and trusting attitudes and conditions are created to know whether our gift is being received.

Barriers to Gift-Giving

A few warnings about gift-giving: First, if we value our reward more than we value the other person, we are demonstrating that we value "things" more than people. When a reward is the goal, the person receiving the gift becomes secondary. Second, pride is a barrier to gift-giving. Pride, the feeling of superiority over others and a contempt or a disdain for them, actually promotes the inequality of the "big me/little you" condition.

Let's consider the example of a woman who is sick. Her family needs help doing the laundry, keeping the children in school, and preparing meals. The father feels harassed and does the best he can, but the family is not coping well. A neighbor sees this condition and wants to help. She goes to the family's home and offers in a kindly way to cook one meal a day for the family and to do the laundry once a week. This is a gift and an act of love. She made the offer because she loves her neighbors and likes the good feelings that come from sharing.

Now let's complicate the picture. Because the sick woman's family is very impressed with their good neighbor, they tell others about it, bragging about what a wonderful neighbor she is. Soon, simple gift-giving produces an external reward of admiration for the giving neighbor.

Secondary rewards and recognitions are flattering and pleasurable, and most of us want them. Some even develop a hunger for them. The neighbor in the above example received not only the simple benefit of returned and shared meaning, but reward and praise as well. She was doubly rewarded and she liked it. But the recognition she received changed her motivation for gift-giving.

In similar situations, if we receive a lot of praise for our good deeds, we may begin to keep score and no longer offer our gifts unconditionally but rather for the purpose of receiving rewards. This type of attitude diminishes the value of gift-giving; it makes us hypocritical and phony and splits us apart. Mutual enhancement does not occur, the other people involved lose their importance, and exterior rewards become paramount. Instead of communicating in a whole, straight, congruent way, we start seeking more rewards. When the rewards become more important than the people we are serving, the integrity and simplicity of the gift is destroyed.

The more the need for an external reward is fed, the more it must be fed. An endless cycle of seeking praise or superiority or public acclaim begins that can have no peaceful, well-integrated end. Unfortunately, the more external rewards we receive, the more we may seek, long for, and crave them. Yet such rewards, like material possessions, lead to emptiness, not fulfillment. Listen to the famous who have lost their fame as they speak of heartbreak. Such people often experience great pain when they lose public acclaim and fortune. Many such people do not have the character to withstand this loss and are unable to see that it was a superficial loss. Love/trust people will not be pulled into the false arena of external reward to begin with. They will follow the fulfilling path of service because they are motivated by love.

After people have found the loving life, they begin to reach out. They get involved, not because it is a good way to belong to a group, but because they want to share. They know they can't solve all the problems of the world, but they dive in where they can help and pursue the greater task. It is as natural for their internal rightness to produce meaningful service as it is for green shoots of maize to produce golden ears of corn.

The Gifts We Inherit

Taking Inventory

Gift-giving has broader dimensions than simple, one-to-one interchanges. We each inherit a powerful, wide variety of gifts from our parents, country, culture, faith, religion, and forebears.

These invisible gifts are all part of the cultural and social heritage we receive as a birthright. We say these gifts are invisible because we take them for granted. But the love/trust person is aware of them and appreciates their great value and the fantastic price paid by those who gave these gifts. An appreciation and an awareness of these wondrous gifts is a gift we give to ourselves, for when we appreciate the past, we place new value on those who have given so much. We also understand the meaning of the gifts we can give to future generations by dealing well with our present.

We were born at the crest of a time wave, a moving mountain of myth and manners, music and morals, machines and mathematics. This is a time of ideas and ideals, of language and learning, schools and society, professions and policies, hospitals and highways. It is everything we would miss if our minds were emptied and we were placed naked in nature. First, let us accept the gifts of the past.

We have inherited good public schools, good roads to drive on, and fire and police protection. We are more confident about our civil rights than were our ancestors. If something is wrong with the system, we can generally change it.

We inherited all of these benefits from our ancestors, many of whom made hard choices and did backbreaking labor to build our society as it is today. Beyond duty, we owe them deep gratitude for what they have given us. For me, the best inheritance I have is my hope, my optimism, and my belief that I can continually make my life more complete, more fully alive and free.

Take a moment to review what you have received as an inheritance from your country, community, family, and church, and from others who have had a significant impact in your life. Think what your life would be like if your parents or grandparents had not immigrated to America a generation or two ago? What kind of personal price did they pay to come here? Were they indentured servants or slaves? Were they the poor in a society in which they could not possibly advance? How would your life be different if you lived in Europe, Asia, or Africa? Consider what it means today to be living in a basically free society with civil rights and liberties, in a society in which you have protections against false accusations and imprisonment. Are you aware that the hard choices and hard work of many generations of forefathers have given you the marvelous opportunities for self-growth that you now enjoy?

Sharing What We've Received

As we become aware of the advantages brought about by our heritage, we will develop a wonderful quieting and deepening of the spirit. Gratitude for our gifts will strengthen our roots and trunk. Too many of us are concerned with our leaves and branches—the fragile aspects of our lives which do not last. Awareness and deep gratitude help to build character; they strengthen us against the fury of the storms of life.

If we want to share the gifts of our culture, we must take advantage of these systems and enhance them in some way as we pass them on to another generation. In my chosen profession, I can help to enhance our understanding of human dynamics and relationships. You may enhance science, literature, music, art, law, child development, medicine, or any area of your expertise and pass it on to others.

I pass on these gifts in many ways. I learn their value, and after I attempt to improve on these gifts I pass them on to my children and grandchildren. My children's gift back to me is to accept that inheritance, to appreciate it, to enjoy it, and to find fulfillment in it. Then they search for and find their own meaning in that context.

Focusing on What We Can Control

A word of caution is in order here: no society is perfect. Cultural weaknesses and shortcomings do exist and must be seen and recognized for what they are. We need to understand those weaknesses and compensate for the damage they do. Our society, for example, is often superficial and its members are not as thoughtful or as caring as they could be. They often emphasize doing and having above being. Though there is vast room for improvement, I believe, from my limited experience, that ours is the healthiest society that I know.

It is never helpful to expect perfection, blame, or condemn whatever society we may live in. We must build on that society's strengths, not focus on its weaknesses. We can neutralize the shortcomings and build a good life around what we can control.

Many factors and situations over which we have no control affect our lives. We cannot change what the president of our country does or what Congress decides (though we may have some influence through occasional letters or visits). We can complain, be angry, and harp about the decisions that those in power make, but such behavior does not change those actions and decisions. What we can always change is our attitudes about them. We can distinguish that which is helpful from that which is harmful in our society, and at key moments, we can learn to choose that which is healthy, build on our strengths, and downplay the rest. This process is one of the advantages of the gift of choice.

When we attempt to manipulate things over which we have no control, we feel powerless, discouraged, and frustrated. We need to carefully delineate that which truly is in our control and that which is not and refuse to waste our energies on situations outside our sphere of influence. This quote says it well:

"God, give us the grace to accept with serenity the things that cannot be changed, courage to change the things which should be changed, and the wisdom to distinguish the one from the other."

Love and Nature's Gifts

In addition to complex social structure, we have inherited a whole world full of beauty. Love, while it is primarily shared between humans, eventually spreads far beyond the human dimension to nature, animals, and to the divine. One can learn to value persons or objects because of the powerful awareness they awaken and the mutual sharing they provide. One evening, as I spent a few hours at the foot of the Tetons, I wrote the following:

Grand Tetons

Tonight, I sit here, a solitary figure
Alone, not alone.
Impressed, aware, inspired, filled, overpowered,
Even intimidated by such a place

Aware of my nothingness.
A solitary figure among these mountains of stone.
But somehow, rather hopeful—
Perhaps a dream lurks here tonight.
A dream I find, lose, find again.
I sit at the feet of the Grand Tetons
And daylight is dying
And these cathedrals
Show me their thousandth face.
The movement of the sun,
The endless panorama of clouds against those faces.
The rugged monoliths of nine million years
So permanent, so secure, so formidable in presence,
Play against my mortal, changing, shifting mood
And I read my finiteness against their infinity—
My fragile hold on life or so it seems in this place.
And tonight I hope my dream will be born again.
And I will be a man to match these mountains.

Coldness descends within my bones
My awkwardness is stark reminder of my humanness,
The sun goes down and I no longer have light and warmth,
And life could end so quickly—
No man knows his day or hour, but it will always be short
But the mountain simply IS
With the old snow mixing with the new
Clouds alternately fluffy, playful, light,
Cold, windy and forbidding—
The endless mix of beauty.
Sky, stone, clouds' patterns changing so fast
No painter could capture their likeness.
But I, cold and numb
Must soon search for warmth and light
And I say to these mountains
You have blessed me
And thrilled me
Shown me grandeur, majesty, perhaps elegance.
But I must know Grand Tetons

It is in me
In all my finiteness
That lies the capacity to know that you are Grand
You know no such thing.
It is in some infinitely remarkable being—such as mine
That intelligence and awareness lie,
That imagination and remembrance live.
And my body the remarkable system of systems
Keeps me alive
To know you.
So in a prayer here tonight, at your feet
My whole being ascends
In majestic gratitude to you—
But more to that God who made us both.

—C. Kay Allen

A New Level of Appreciation

As we experience any inspiring scene in nature, we can be awed by its magnificence and the powerful feelings created in us. Our increased awareness of the beauty of the mountains or the ocean opens up a vista of appreciation. We glory in that beauty, marvelling at its grandeur, and as that appreciation grows, we become increasingly aware of our own value, who we are and our place in the universe. We can feel a oneness with the mountain that whispers to our souls—we share a part of something great, glorious and somehow divine.

We choose our response to beauty as a result of the way we view the world. A person at the fear/anxiety level sees a beautiful sunset and it means nothing to him: "Let's get on with life" is his attitude. At the duty/justice level, he sees the same sunset for a brief moment and says, "Oh, isn't that pretty." At the love/trust level, he may sit and watch it for an hour, awed by the colors, the clouds forming and reforming over the mountain peaks, and the brilliant flaming ball of the sun.

This glorious appreciation at the love/trust level is a gift that is not received by the fear/anxiety person. He denies this gift to himself, although he is unaware that he is making that denial. It flows halfway through the duty/justice level, but all the way through at love/trust. Sharing with nature and appreciation of God's handiwork enriches us at this level in such a way that we not only feel harmony with nature, but experience the oneness of all creation. And yet, the perceptions and feelings that truly appreciate nature are not "out there"—they are inside, all within us.

What gift does nature give to us? As I look out the windows this morning, I see aspen trees slowly swaying in the wind. I see the spruce trees with snow on their branches, and that snow occasionally drops through to the ground below. My heart responds to the wondrous beauty of the scene. I love being here. I am glad that what I see is not an ugly scene, a garbage dump, or a horrible war scene. I am aware that I chose to come to a place where there would be natural beauty. I feel full, warm, and trusting. These powerful feelings are triggered and enhanced by the mountains, the sunset or the sea. They are accepted and appreciated within me, and I feel the wondrous gift of oneness.

We give nature meaning as a result of our appreciation. It is enhanced as we glory in it, and the enjoyment we feel enriches our meaning. Our appreciation is our gift to nature.

The love that is shared between humans and animals is a similar type of gift. For example, our friends have a tiny poodle. He is like a person to them, a member of the family. When they have been apart it is fun to see their reunion. The dog runs around, scampering over the rugs and furniture, shedding pleasure (and hair!) on everyone and everything. The delight is shared by his masters. Unquestionably they give gifts to each other.

Life itself eventually becomes a constant state of enhancement through gift-giving and receiving—a love affair with the mountains, the sea, the grain fields, and with those portions of nature that enrich our lives. The pleasure, excitement, and devotion that we feel toward all nature and every animal also increases our ability to love. We feel "at one" with all our world, a oneness which takes us to the very threshold of our final way of love.

THE FIFTH WAY OF LOVE: ONENESS AND HARMONY

The fifth way of love is this: *From the enhancement and growth of sharing comes a new awareness: "I am not and cannot be complete alone." The human family needs each other in order to discover meaning. It is in living in harmony that we discover the beauty within ourselves, the joy we share with our significant others, and the love found throughout God's universe.*

We share the best within us and see beneath the surface to the best in others. The endless quest for greater understanding leads us to transcend the self and learn the meaning of the oneness that Christ prayed for: "That they all may be one; as thou, Father, art in me, and I in thee, that they also may be one in us." (John 17:21.) Love and life are sacred, and we live to experience their oneness.

Introduction

Occasionally we experience magic moments in life. Everything seems perfect, right here, right now. One such time, for many of us, is our first experience with being "in love." Another magic moment often occurs when our first child is born, and we gaze in awe at the reality of new life, at incredibly tiny fingers and blissful innocence. The miracle is not lessened by the fact that it has happened billions of times before; indeed, that fact is rarely even noticed in the rapture of realizing that we have played a crucial role in this present miracle—we are now co-creators of a brand new person. Most of us feel an urge to pray in thanksgiving for the wonder of it all.

Occasionally, death is such a time too. When a great life's work has been done well, and only suffering remains, release from the cares of this world brings relief and peace—not only to the sojourner but to all those who have cared for the person who has gone on. If we are to believe the many reports of near-death experiences published in recent years, the transition process between this life and the next is a pleasant, even exhilarating, experience.

Magic moments of harmony can happen in other ways as well. We may struggle for months to say what is truly in our hearts and find our efforts yielding only awkward words, dead feelings, and emotional emptiness. Then we will suddenly find our words springing to life, taking wings and expressing more than words can, granting freedom to the secrets hiding in the soul.

We can even be transported to a higher realm of living and being in solitude. This is sometimes achieved by meditation, prayer, communion with nature, artistic expression or athletic achievement, and sometimes by struggling through a trial until the light pierces the gloom.

It is difficult to define oneness and harmony. We can taste it in degrees, and whether we get a morsel or a feast, we know instantly that harmony is the elixir we have sought since the beginning. And we know we want it again.

The Savior repeatedly acknowledged his oneness with the Father—"I and my Father are one" (John 10:30)—and lovingly but firmly taught that there should be unity and oneness among his disciples—"There shall be one fold, and one shepherd. (John 10:16.)

In modern scripture, the Savior also said this: "And if ye are not one ye are not mine."

Apostle Paul further witnessed and promised that seeking harmony with others would bring harmony within: "Be of one mind . . . and the God of love and peace shall be with you." (2 Corinthians 13:11.)

Accepting others invites our union with them and fosters individual inner harmony and the peace of oneness within.

A Wider Vision of Oneness and Harmony

Listening to Your Inner Voice

For many years I was too busy with my business interests to pay much attention to my inner voice. In truth, I was afraid of what I might hear if I did listen. "Freud is right," my fears whispered, "the deepest truth in the human psyche is the death wish." To avoid falling into the feared bottomless inner pool, I made myself "too busy" to look for it.

But one can only avoid that search for so long. In time I had to make my way through several ordeals. In the process, I had some deep bedrock experiences with myself. I did go deeper, past my fears, and eventually came to my deepest affirmations. I know now we need fear no inner evil, for there is no evil to fear. When we finally confront the beast in the cage, we find the cage empty. This discovery was an ecstatic surprise for me.

The new confidence I gained from my journeys within myself allowed me to merge the inner self and the outer self. This integration of personhood is the basis of an all-encompassing harmony I have enjoyed a few precious times in my life, and which serves me well as a source of strength and comfort.

At the time of this writing, I had experienced two quadruple bypass operations and survived ten heart attacks. Prior to the latest series of coronary attacks, I was heavily involved in several real estate developments, numerous banking ventures, and had founded and was directing both the Human Development Institute and the Human Values Institute. Each endeavor exacted its toll in energy, time, commitment, and money, and I often felt harassed by all the reality problems and logistical demands, including a prolonged real estate recession in Denver.

But now I know better ways to handle stress, to quiet the outer voice and trust the inner. When I am discouraged, I retreat to a quiet place in nature and go within. Soon it becomes clear the core problem is with me, not "out there." When I listen to the inner voice, reverberating gently with the pure tones of personal affirmation, I can then go back to the real world and speak moderately, helpfully, and trustfully to my associates, congruent with what is in my heart.

After this refreshment, this little drink from the clear waters, my natural tendency to blame others dries up. Then it is easier to see disrespect as the damning viewpoint that it is and to see that disagreement does not justify disrespect. Instead of more divisions and hostility, I find compatibility and solutions. As usual, these external results flow directly from my deepest self. My intent has changed—instead of competition, I seek cooperation.

Sensitivity to the inner voice is partly a matter of listening without fear and hearing without argument. But it is also a more general attitude. It is taking time to smell the roses. It is knowing that a whisper penetrates deeper than a shout. It is touching lightly instead of clinging tightly. It is the simple gift, the homemade heart.

Other Ideas of Oneness

The Peak Experience

We have seen consistently that most self-discovery proceeds gradually in a steady pattern of progression from one level of discipline and maturation to the next, interspersed with new insights, lengthened perspective, and rekindled hope. But there is another factor in the the development of personal growth which modern psychologists call the *peak experience*—the sudden and usually unexpected transcendence of the normal. My discussion of the peak experience is based on the work of Abraham Maslow (particularly from his book *Religions, Values, and Peak Experiences*), from insights shared with me by my friends and acquaintances who have received this ultimate gift, and from my own experiences.

Although the term "peak experience" is relatively new, the experience itself is not. Several of these peak experiences have been major turning points in history. Though they come down to us in the coats of many cultures, there is a common essence to them. They include Moses' refining before the burning bush, the enlightenment of Buddha, the revelation of Mohammed, the transfiguration of Christ, and Paul's conversion on the road to Damascus. The *satori* of the Zen master and the trance of the Hopi medicine man seem likely to be other forms of the peak experience. Nearly all religions are based on some transcendent insight given to or thrust upon a founder or a prophet. In the case of the transfiguration of Christ, the whole process was long foretold by prophecy.

Peak experiences provide an overwhelming transformation of outlook and bring a completely new frame of reference. When we attempt to understand this concept from our normal state of mind, we are at a distinct disadvantage because understanding is based on language, and language is symbolic. But in such a transcendent state, there is no symbolism, there are no words.

Transcendence is the grand present tense. In the transcendent state, everything is direct, immediate, pure, and now. All becoming and doing are suddenly pure being—radiant, and all-engrossing. Transcendence is absolutely involving. Everything that we have perceived as separate parts of us, such as mind, body, soul, and intellect, are totally melded into a whole without parts. It is not a mixture, but a melt. Time and space are perceived differently, as a single continuum. At this level, infinity and eternity seem understandable and accessible. Life is inherently good and is felt to be so. Life needs no purpose, for purposes are separate reasons for living. Life is self-validating. We experience awe at the wonder of it all. The majesty of creation is one sweeping insight which generates profound gratitude. We experience a sense of peace and confidence that all creation is in unison.

We cannot make peak experiences happen; they are gifts, not rewards that we earn or achieve. We cannot deliberately invoke them. Though it is possible to have such experiences at any level of living, they are much more frequent among people who are approaching or living the love/trust life. They are most common during or shortly after a grinding tribulation; however, trials alone will certainly not make them happen. But whatever the depth or duration of a peak experience, the recipient is nearly always left deeply moved and fundamentally changed. The newly defined world view deflates whatever urge for contention that may remain. We feel naturally drawn toward love and unity. Controlling other people is no longer attractive. We release *having* values and *being* values settle in. We strive to develop equal relationships, not out of altruism, but out of spontaneous desire. Constants are accepted as they are. Fear is seen for what it is and does, and then it is cleared. Fear, seen now as the absence of love, can be removed. John tells us "perfect love casteth out fear." (1 John 4:18.) To the truest believers, all the facts are friendly.

"I-Thou" Versus "I-It" Relationships

Other major, but not commonly discussed, ideas about unity and oneness are well worth considering. One of the most profound of these is the philosophy of contemporary philosopher Martin Buber.

Austrian-born Buber developed the concept of "I-Thou" and "I-It" relationships. These phrases describe two different ways in which we can look at the world. I-Thou, which Buber calls the primary relationship, is based on unconditional relating, openness, and uniqueness. It signifies respect for an equal, acknowledgement of fellowship, and recognition of worth. In contrast, I-It is the condescending attitude, the relationship of a person to a thing. The thing may be a stone or a machine, or a living being who is treated as a non-living thing.

By Buber's definition, the primary relationship is the source of meaning and the I-It relationship is the source of alienation. I-It fosters tendencies to dominate, control, and manipulate, as the insecure "I" seeks validation through power over the yielding "It," whether it is a piece of clay or a person treated like dirt. The "I" seeks worth by elevating himself above other things. The net result is a consciousness of separations, divisions, and conflict. The dominating "I" does not find the confirmation he seeks, for the more he treats others as lifeless things, the more dead he feels inside. As he makes a high pyramid of things under his control and rises on its peak, he finds himself increasingly isolated, more barren, and profoundly lonely.

I-Thou is the method of relating with others center to center, person to person, sovereign to sovereign. This mutual respect creates a new entity—"Us"—which is the combination of what each has to offer to the relationship. "Us" is a source of joy, meaning, and strength, for each partner may draw from "us" something greater than themselves and still not diminish the combination. If we are to avoid being split internally, we must become one with our environment. If this unity is to be uplifting, it must be on a basis of equality. As our essence and divine legacy are the same as that of our fellow beings, using them as a means to our own ends only debases our own value, symbolically converting us into mere stepping stones, too.

A common example of the I-It attitude is the fear which most people have of snakes, bugs, and spiders—the creepy crawly things. As we learn to relate in an I-Thou way to these co-citizens of nature, we grow beyond disgust to appreciation, and see them not as enemies but as creatures who are, like us, living out their design.

The Challenge of Attaining "I-Thou"

One basic reason we have trouble attaining the I-Thou attitude so essential to the feeling of harmony in our lives is that our thought patterns are formed by the structure of our language. English grammar is fundamentally based on subject acting upon subject, or in other words, the I-It relationship. Without this one-thing-is-doing-something-to-another-thing form, we have incomplete sentences, improper grammar, and riled English teachers.

In contrast to this mode of thought is the structure of many Asian languages, where there is little concern for the complete sentence. We can see this plainly in the Japanese art of haiku poetry, where a series of short word phrases, sometimes logically unconnected, is used to paint a sparse and still picture, or perhaps to set up a mood, but rarely does it express action. A typical haiku line might refer to "A green tree," and reading it, we would ask, "Well, what about the green tree? What is it doing, what is going to happen to it? What is its function in this scene?" But the essence of this art form is not what is done to or by the tree, but simply the green tree *being* a green tree, and that is all. When translated into English, these poems are sometimes given verbs and connecting thoughts to make them less enigmatic to the Western mind, but in the original they tend to be emotional flash cards.

There is, I suspect, a modern tendency toward greater acceptance of the incomplete sentence, the unrhymed poem, the painting that counterbalances intense color with nearly empty space, the asymmetrical building, and the orchestral piece that "floats" more than goes somewhere. Such developments indicate that our society is beginning to transcend the limitations of traditional grammar-based thought patterns and to think more in the I-Thou frame of mind and reference.

I-Thou relationships are based on unconditional relating. They are open, equal, and accepting. The loving person sees other people, all living things, ultimately everything, as "thou," the respected equal.

The Yin-Yang Symbol of Unity

To the loving person, unity is the basis of reality. The old opposites are resolved, sometimes by placing polar extremes on a continuum, sometimes by seeing them as complements rather than enemies. This concept is beautifully represented in the ancient Chinese Yin/Yang symbol. It is the circle divided into two teardrop-shaped halves, always shown in contrasting light and dark colors.

The two light and dark regions are called the yin and the yang. Yin represents what the Chinese traditionally call the feminine or passive principles of nature, including coldness, wetness, and darkness. In contrast, the yang signifies the traditionally aggressive or male aspects of nature, such as light, heat, and dryness. In Chinese thought these two extremes must combine to produce anything which is to be, and this procreative combination is represented by a seed. For in the very center of each region there is a small dot representing the seed of its opposite. The idea is not that each extreme contains the seed of its own destruction, but rather that it contains the essence of its complement, the beginning of its completion.

In the enlightened view of oneness and harmony, all the old opposites lose their stridency as diametric absolutes. Women and men are not opposites but two equally necessary parts whose union creates future humanity. Such seeming opposites as life and death are not really contrary; death is a only a leap (although a quantum leap) in the larger plan of life. Cold is not the opposite of heat but only the relative absence of it, and nowhere in the universe is heat absolutely absent. The desert and the ocean each have their roles to play in the cycles of nature. The more we accept the gestalt (or integrated structure) of our own being, the more we will see the common essence underlying all apparent contradictions.

Achieving Harmony by Discovering Bedrock

Another deeper, more powerful and more permanent experience awaits us in a path we can choose and control—the search for the deepest levels of bedrock.

Bedrock: A Solid Foundation, a Chosen Path

The geological definition of bedrock is a solid foundation on which to build. This definition also applies for our purposes. Finding individual bedrock and finding bedrock in a relationship gives us a solid foundation on which to build harmony in our lives. Bedrock is a safe place because at bedrock all pretense is gone. Bedrock does not demand perfection but simply demands that we be real. Bedrock is based on integrity and honesty. It has nothing to do with what you have or what you do—only what you are.

While the peak experience often comes as a gift, discovering deeper levels of bedrock requires effort, and is within each person's ability to achieve. This process of discovery involves both our good works and the grace of God at necessary times. It is the process that each of us can choose as we move up the ladder to our own destiny. It is neither a simple gift nor an accident; it is a chosen path.

The Spiritual Nature of Bedrock

Learning self-acceptance and implementing powerful positive affirmations about ourselves will help lead us to the harmony of bedrock. Achieving the bedrock of trust—with other people, with ourselves, or with the Lord—requires that we abandon all pretense and operate at the highest levels of integrity. Deep bedrock is essentially spiritual in nature or at least consists of spiritual overtones or elements. When this level of bedrock is reached, the realization prevails that something infinitely important has happened.

Personal bedrock may be experienced at the moment of conversion when one is convinced that God exists and loves each of us, and there is no further need to question that issue. Bedrock moments may occur when a deep conviction is obtained that Jesus the Christ is a personal Savior who marks one's path or at the moment of realization of how deeply committed one is to his religion.

Bedrock Turning Points

The creation of bedrock may be a significant turning point, giving us confidence to move in a new or more positive direction. An experience from my personal life may illustrate.

I had recently accepted a position of leadership in my church. I had accepted this particular calling with the singles program rather dutifully, and for the first few months I didn't enjoy it much. One evening I was walking in the downtown central part of Denver where our church building was located. I decided to go into the building and simply began walking through every room quietly in the dark until I reached the darkened chapel where I felt the strong need to pray. In the midst of that prayer I was suddenly immersed in the most comforting and warm feeling of love and serenity that I have ever experienced. I knew at that moment that my calling with the singles was the right place for me at that time; I was doing what I was supposed to be doing. My whole being changed and from that moment on I loved every phase of that assignment with single adults. I found it easy to love and accept them, to cry with them, mourn with them, and share their burdens.

Bedrock and the Love/Trust Life

For most of us, a bedrock experience is our first taste of true being, our first experience with the love/trust life. When living in fear, we shout our threats; when driven by duty, we discuss our bargains; when in the bedrock of trust, we speak our meaning quietly in slow, penetrating speech laced with eloquent silences.

Honest self-acceptance is the pathway to the most profound bedrock, a most flowing reception "back home." The commitments you make to yourself during these private bedrock experiences can be the most solid commitments you will ever make. From such deep internal revelations you will find it easier and more comfortable to be authentic, self-controlling, and self-correcting. You will develop a powerful ability to recognize and eliminate negative attitudes and harmful behaviors, and you will come to experience inner joy.

Clear Self-Definition and Personal Bedrock

One of the greatest personal powers we can achieve through bedrock experiences is to clearly define our spiritual, real selves and our true, unchanging values so that we can boldly, strongly talk back to the "alternative voices" in our minds. The battle that goes on in each person's mind and heart is largely between the true voices of the spirit and false voices that seek to thwart, discourage, deceive, and destroy us. However, once we have reached bedrock with ourselves and God in any area, we can never again be deceived for long—we will soon recognize and be able to talk back to those insidious voices in our minds and turn them off. We come to know on a deep level that self-acceptance is life and light, and self-rejection is death and darkness. Our choice is clear and we choose the light joyously.

Over the last two years I have counseled with a woman recovering from a devastating divorce, as well as other significant trials in her life. She accepted the challenge to take responsibility for the quality of her life and her own personal happiness. She told me that as she searched her soul, meditated, and prayed for direction, she would drive to the edge of the Colorado prairie and walk its windswept breadth in solitude for hours. Using this setting to describe the "late afternoon" of her spiritual life, an unmistakable turning point, she shares the following poem which is symbolic of one of her deepest bedrock experiences.

Late Afternoon

Alone on windswept prairie beneath cathedral sky,
I search the wide horizon for chariots of fire
but meet only purple mountains majesty,
and billowing white clouds,
Taunting distant thunder and backdrop
for dancing brown-eyed Susans
and the steadfast nodding sunflowers,
Determined to brighten these searing hours
and decorate rippling amber waves,
providing cover for my surrendered sins
buried here in shallow graves.

An unlikely setting for sacred grove or epiphany,
this barren Gethsemane so far from Jordan,
no sound remaining except the wind
and trill of meadowlark
Who dares to sing and pierce parched air,
hiding in tangled grasses
among wild goldenrod and thistle,
my sole companion and willing witness to
Altared anguish and sacraments in this
crucible of loneliness and forty days of wilderness,
the victory not yet won.

Then in angled light of waning afternoon
I share another's presence,
Enfolded in His grace and mercy,
understanding now complete.
There will be no marbled walls or mirrored halls

in this temple of my tempering
Where I bring as offering my acquiescence soul-deep
and abdication of desires,
Whispering, "Not my will, but thine be done."
I will lift up mine eyes unto the hills.
                                        —Lea Diane Engebretsen

In the scriptural account recorded by Luke we read of Christ's visit
to Bethany, to the home of Mary and Martha, sisters of the Lazarus
whom Christ raised from the dead. Mary, we are told, "sat at Jesus'
feet, and heard His word," while Martha—anxiously engaged in
meal preparation—was dismayed that her sister was not helping.
From her bedrock of deepest understanding, Mary knew what was
most important. She had so internalized her own truest need and the
Savior's truest need—which was not for temporal sustenance or
food but for those who would hear and implement His words of eternal life—that Christ recognized her motive and acknowledged her
gift: "Mary hath chosen that good part, which shall not be taken
away from her." (Luke 10:39, 42.)

At the deepest level of our being comes the firm conviction that
we are actually the Lord's work and His glory, and that all of his
commandments are inherently spiritual and for our individual
growth. There is no more guessing. We know God knows we are
here, and that He knows and understands us, and we can now rejoice
with Isaiah: "And the Lord shall guide thee continually, and satisfy
thy soul in drought . . . and thou shalt be like a watered garden, and
like a spring of water, whose waters fail not. (Isaiah 58:11.) By turning our lives over to Him, we are healed. We are one with Him.

Living the Love/Trust Life

The Untapped Market—Mankind's Search for the Holy Grail

When moviemakers and TV producers are asked why they don't
portray the good side of life or journalists are asked why they report
primarily bad news, the reply is usually to the effect that only conflict arouses interest and that most people find good news propagan-
distic. If this view accurately reflects the tastes of most consumers,
it only indicates how little experience we have with the feelings of

personal integration and the inklings of greatness that lie dormant within. For once these urges are awakened, they become the most powerful forces in human motivation.

I believe evil and conflict are not necessary for interest. The media would discover an untapped market if they would stir the inner depth and portray mankind's search for the Holy Grail (and occasionally they do). In over twenty years of speaking to highly diverse groups, I have never seen people bored by a call to better their lives. If the majority really is uninterested in the uplifting, it is partly because our mass media emphasize low-level attitudes that tend to numb us to our higher possibilities and keep us addicted to the idea that happiness is external.

Self-Enhancement through Giving

As we become actualizers, we are anything but numb, and although joy is our object we do not seek it directly. We share our meaning through giving, working, and serving, and love and joy are the natural by-products. As givers we have learned the great secret: as we give we are enhanced by the giving. It is not the absorption of adoration that satisfies our universal hunger. It is the outpouring of compassion that delivers the great payoff—those times of closeness, wholeness, oneness. It is the sharing process that ties us together, that manifests our unity and fulfills the deepest hunger.

Merging the Ideal and the Real

In the state of *being*, we move beyond the entropic life where we start dying as soon as we are born, where everything is always running down and getting worse, and where Murphy's pessimistic "laws" explain it all. In this state, we rise above the judgmental, differential, oppositional way of seeing the world. *Being* is joyful acceptance of our place in the whole divine plan.

When we are close to or in the *being* state, we no longer worry about having the skill to listen, or whether we are listening well. Now we simply *are* a safe place to be, as listening is an inseparable aspect of our nature. We no longer concern ourselves with honesty, for it is so ingrained that we cannot be dishonest. The time of separations fades away. The ideal person and the real person are now one. The lesser selves are now merged into the greater selves.

A Day in the Love/Trust Life

Let us walk through a typical day with a person who is living the love/trust life. I tell the story of a day in the love/trust life from the perspective of a professional male only because that is what I know; certainly there are appropriate versions for others. I have also related it from the viewpoint of an older person because, in general, it takes a long time to "get it together."

• Awake and Alive!

As he slowly drifts back into shore from a night of sailing on the sea of dreams, he relishes the remaining surreal pictures and wonders about their meaning. The last images float away, and he begins forming visions of the real day ahead. It is a gradual, easy, pleasant process, just as the restful night of sleep has been. Later he will rejoin the alarm clock world of civilized man, but for now he prefers to be the "primitive man," and lets the busy birds outside his open window gently coax him from his slumber with a song.

After he has allowed consciousness to reclaim him, he turns the radio on to find out how the world is doing. As his feet hit the floor he wiggles his toes on the carpet and slides his feet back and forth for a good morning rub. It feels good. He rolls out and sees his wife still sleeping soundly. He lets her finish the journey at her own pace.

He makes his way to the bathroom, wobbling a little at first. The salivation for fresh orange juice is beginning already, and he enjoys taunting himself a bit with it. He runs his fingers over his overnight beard, proudly inspecting the growth and roughness. Then he splatters the shaving cream all over, flashing back briefly in his mind to the childhood fun of finger paints. He winces and grimaces, twisting and contorting his face to give his razor the ideal angle to harvest the crop. He looks like a slightly berserk mime in the mirror. If the people at the office only knew, he thinks humorously.

In years past he would adjust the shower water and then stand back to avoid being startled by that first nasty spit of cold water from the riser pipe, and then sneak in to the stream after the warm water was flowing. No more. Now he stands directly under the nozzle, pulls the handle straight out and thinks, "Gimme all ya got!"

Dressing for the day ahead, his mind is occupied in planning what to do after the first good impression is made.

Breakfast is simple but wonderful—just a bowl of shredded wheat, bite size, with fresh berries, and a large egg boiled exactly three minutes and twenty-five seconds. Stingy on the salt these days. Then, the prize—the chilled juice of three large, ripe Valencia oranges that he personally sliced right down the middle with his sharpest knife and then pressed on the juicer until they gave up every last drop. *La dolce vita*!

Driving to work, he gets caught in the mass morning migration but thinks little of it. His mind is now rehearsing the day's schedule. There are some unpleasant tasks ahead today, but he is confident he can meet them positively. He is competent and likes the people he works with, and he knows they sense that.

He turns the car radio on, hears a good song and sings along, at least on the chorus. Looking out, he sees not only the cars, he sees the people in them. He smiles at several of them and waves to a few he knows, or would like to know. The trees along the roadside are on duty proudly today and the shrubbery on the median is blooming outrageously, and he notices it all. Off in the distance the mountains loom reassuringly, motionlessly protecting the flatland with thunderous grace. He feels a deep sense of gratitude.

• All in a Day's Work

As he enters the office, coworkers greet him cordially and he returns their smiles and warmth. He is well respected, even by his competitors, yet he is not egotistical. A positive team player, he is willing, even eager, to share the credit for a job well done. He enjoys achievement for its own sake but has little use for plaques, awards, and certificates. Instead, nature scenes and family pictures adorn his office walls.

The first meeting concerns something he knows little about, so he asks only a few questions and mainly listens. He learns some new things and likes that. Then he has an hour alone, and he chips away at the ubiquitous paperwork conspiring to devour his desk. It's not much fun but must be done, so he stoically wades through the stack.

A later meeting doesn't go so well. As disagreement verges on anger, he backs away, takes a deep breath, closes his eyes and concentrates on what is happening. This takes only a second or two, and then he looks his adversary in the eye and says, "I don't like the way this is going. How about you?"

When his coworker replies, "We need to solve this problem," he responds, "Yes, I agree with that. Actually, we agree on a lot of things, don't we?" Slowly he goes deeper, inviting cooperation by emphasizing common ground. The meeting ends without a viable solution, but the air has been cleared and they will make real progress next week. That's just fine for now.

Lunch is with a new colleague, and they are so interested in picking one another's brains, they hardly notice their meal. His colleague, like many people, enjoys his friendship; he is sought out as a friend and confidante because everyone knows he is a good listener, a safe place. He has opinions on almost everything and loves to share them. After doing so, he will listen for another opinion, not to argue, compare, or judge, but just to understand.

He takes some quiet time after lunch. He glances briefly at a trade magazine, then puts it down and simply rests silently—head back and eyes closed, for a few minutes.

During the afternoon a sales presentation becomes tense, and he breaks the tension with a joke. It's easy humor, laughing at himself, but not raining on anyone else's parade.

A new project is proposed in mid-afternoon. He knows he is beginning to tire and doesn't make his best decisions in such a state, so asks to "sleep on it." Profit opportunity no longer has the big draw it used to, so now he waits patiently for the project that has personal meaning for him, recognizing that the means matter at least as much as the end.

A conversation with a fellow worker goes beyond business to personal sharing, and he likes that. They proudly talk about their respective new granddaughter and daughter.

• Home, Sweet Home

When he returns home he is tired but arrives with anticipation and gladness—not too tired for a few quiet words with his wife, and then a romp in the yard with the dog and visiting grandchildren. After a day of talk he finds it refreshing to have an hour of action, and grandchildren know how to provide it!

The sense of contentment he enjoys now is balanced with a greater need to remain aware of the equilibrium between his desire to be socially useful on one hand and his continuing quest for knowledge on the other. These are not sharply drawn distinctions but, rather, needs operating at different times within him. Commercial entertainment is not so important as it once was, and a hectic social life is no longer appealing. Now he and his wife would rather have close friends over to visit for an evening, sit beside the fire together and listen to music, or talk to their grown children on the phone. A good brisk walk seeing all the flowers and well-kept yards seems unusually satisfying. But this has not lessened his desire to learn, to experience the excitement of books and conversation, to share ideas, or to experience new thoughts and emotions. After all these years he is still interested in many things. Some evenings he spends one way and some another, content with all his options.

His physical, intellectual, emotional, and social needs are now answered more simply, without calling in the martyr or the fool. He eats more modestly and does not bemoan what he cannot have. He does what he ought because now he wants to do so. When confronted by a duty, he does it without feeling resentment and then forgets about it.

Later, when he crawls into bed, he curls his toes as he thrusts his feet into the cool sheets and slides his feet back and forth in the bed, enjoying the sensations. Then, the most reliable ritual of his life, that hasn't changed since he was a child—a few minutes reading before the lights go out.

Welcoming his wife to bed with a tender embrace and kiss, he thinks about how their intimacy has grown more precious as it has become less sexual and more quietly talkative. He has decided that there is less need to share the body when the heart is shared so completely.

He is glad she is there. He is glad the years of searching for the ways to make the marriage work have finally born sweet fruit and does not envy the young with their confusion and health, even though he feels his own body slowing and weakening.

But lying quietly in the dark he also realizes that another essential and more vital element has now become an integral part of him. Not only does he feel better about himself and work better with other people, but he has developed a depth of oneness and companionship with this companion of his heart—his wife—that is very safe and feels wonderful to them both. Their relationship encompasses not only mutual trust and love, but seems oceanic in view—that is, the simple things are now more important and predominate. They have reached the pure simplicity beyond complexity.

This sweet simplicity overflows from their relationship to their interaction with others and their joys in the little things of life—simple things like the wonderful feel of water in taking a shower or a cool refreshing drink on a hot day, food tasted in all its marvelous variety, an indescribable sunset shared, or talking with a precious grandchild, watching and awed for the hundredth time how different children learn at different ages.

His life is not boring although it has a different kind of excitement than when he was a younger man. He has troubles and trials now as always, and he tires more easily, aware that serious illness may be a possibility in these later years. But he is neither preoccupied nor unduly concerned; he has long since made peace with his faith that life transcends death—and that death is indeed part of life and need not be feared.

What fears he does have involve his concern for loved ones and family members—anxious that none of them become injured or harmed in any way. But even those possibilities are viewed with some calmness. And when he can't sleep, he is not overly concerned. He simply does what he wants to do until sleep comes—grateful to live in an age where pain need not be all encompassing and devastating.

In contemplative moments, he now realizes that he can truly let go. He does not have to judge himself against a perfect standard. He did what he could do today with a sense of peace—spending the best part of the day in meaningful human relationships that were positive and productive. And he has come to a sense of peace about his God, being able to talk to him and admit truth in his prayers, and finding the comfort that such prayers can provide. He has experienced that "peace that passeth all understanding."

Oneness

With Self

In the Bible we find God defining his nature, his name, and his purpose in terms of being. When Moses inquires of God how he should answer the children of Israel when they asked him the name of God, he is instructed to tell them, "*I AM* hath sent me unto you." (Exodus 3:14.)

As with God, unity is the essential characteristic of the love/trust life. From this point of view we see the world in terms of wholeness, not differences. This is the ultimate in enlightened self-interest, for we see that we are better off integrated than divided, both individually and collectively.

Several years ago I wrote this poem, trying to express the human longing for oneness and harmony.

More Silences

There is a silence in each of you that is yours alone.
There is the silence of learning no one really understands.
The shocked silence of knowing you must stand alone
in every key moment.

There is the silence of friendship gone dead,
When, after so much to say,
there is nothing left to say.
There is the silence of wanting to explain,
when all the words sound cold or lifeless,
and silence freezes the feelings.
And in these silences,
you know words only imprison you
in a deeper silence.

There is the silence of your secret fears,
buried in your deepest chamber,
the desperate hope no one sees the tattered lining
in your coat.
There is the silence of uncertainty,
when others seem to know,
but you do not.
And there is the silence more still,
which says you are a searcher, a seeker, a pilgrim:
it is not for you to know.

There will be more silences, the silence of broken love,
when the ways which seemed so open and beautiful
have closed down,

and your life lies shattered at your feet.
There will be the silence of great fear,
binding you to the deadness of your lesser self,
saying, "You do not matter."
There will be the dreaded silence which says
the cynics are right,
and when you die that is the end,
there is nothing left.

There will be a welcome silence, too,
a silence whispering love,
where no uttered sound can capture the joy, the wholeness,
the oneness;
When only you and your Maker can sense
the infinite within you,
the everlasting possibilities that now lie
a sleeping giant within,
slowly asking to be awakened by the fires of love.
And the deepest silence,
affirming that God is there,
He understands.

He will hear you when you pay the price,
when you relinquish your will,
when your silent prayer humbly says "Thy will . . . "
Then He will mold and fashion you in His own image,
male and female,
and it will be very good.
You will feel the silence echoing within
as you realize you are the Creator's masterpiece,
the last word.

The silence will open, and you will know you are His child.
The silence will flow,
and you will see there is no end to you.
The silence will fill you,
and you will live and love forever.

With Others

We all have the potential to live the love/trust life—a life based on acceptance of ourselves and others. As we embrace ourselves in the process of self-acceptance, we become conscious of an increased desire for and awareness of our obligation to seek unity and harmony with all others, that we may "stand fast in one spirit, with one mind." (Philippians 1:27.) We begin to understand that "we, being many, are one body in Christ, and every one members one of another." (Romans 12:5.) We begin to internalize the connection between that great commandment "Love thy neighbor" and its tremendously significant contingency clause, "as thyself."

In this state of being, the very way in which we see the world changes. The people who are special to us are seen as essential parts of our world. But beyond that we see, perhaps for the first time, even our enemies as fellow creatures who may also feel lonely and misunderstood. The poor waif is not seen as a dirty, disgusting child but as an innocent victim of circumstance whose scruffiness is only a thin shell waiting to be cracked by a fearless and tender hand. St. Francis counted as a turning point in his life the day he was revulsed by the leper and passed him by. Then St. Francis rebuked himself for unfaithfulness to his Exemplar and returned to kiss the diseased hand and fill it with coins.

Today literal lepers and street urchins are more rare, but the cries for help are greater than ever. Many of us develop intricate denial routines to ignore the cries and to insulate ourselves from the need: "Don't tell me your troubles, I got troubles of my own." But as we become love/trust people, we do just the opposite. We know that the child in the abusive home, the father addicted to alcohol, the unmarried pregnant teenager, the immigrant locked out by language, the adolescent lost in search of self and afraid to trust anyone, the widowed grandmother out of money, the refugee out of hope, and the patient out of time are all brothers and sisters. Each of them is a part of us. We do not choose up sides or blame. Our hearts may be sick for the abused child, but they are equally sick for the abusive parent.

When we live the fearful life we avoid the cries. When we live the dutiful life we patronize the helpless and take pride in our little contributions. But in the loving life we know and acknowledge, "There but for the grace of God go I." Rather than avoid all the signals, loving people fine-tune their sensitivity, respond to the need, and seek out service opportunities to best use their unique abilities. People who are enlightened see more than a world in need of love; they see a world they need to love.

With God

God is love. As we become one with Him, we are complete. In those moments we are at the deepest bedrock. We know what He wants for us and that He is in a working relationship with us. We know that we are not complete without him.

And now our understanding comes full circle as we begin to see others through the eyes of love and trust, as God sees them. We are enhanced in a thousand ways, no longer wanting to be hurtful or harmful, no longer envious, covetous, competitive, or self-serving. As we thus embrace the center of ourselves, we achieve that oneness with God and Jesus that the Savior prayed for when he said, "That they all may be one; as thou, Father, art in me, and I in thee." If we love one another, God dwelleth in us, and his love is perfected in us. (John 17:21.) There is no greater oneness. There is no greater joy. And it is found in living "The Ways and Power of Love."

Strong Enough to Love

Love is the passport to oneness and harmony and requires strength. Love is being strong enough to accept another person unconditionally, to be a safe harbor for them. Love is being strong enough to take the anger and hostility out of the hostile situation. Love is being strong enough to build trust by confrontation when necessary. Love is being strong enough to find the bedrock of trust.

What does it take to break through the barriers of telestial and terrestrial living to a place where we see all of our options instead of all of our limits—to a place where our feelings of grandeur, joy, awe, and gratitude transform every simplicity into richness, every relationship into something deeper than we had imagined, every song into a song of praise? What does it take to find such joy in the little things and regular routines of daily life?

It takes going through all the learning and growth stages described in this book. It takes our willingness to acknowledge the universal hunger for love and to define the growth process in realistic terms.

It takes our daring to make the journey within, learn honest self-acceptance, and increase our awareness.

It takes our perseverance in practicing the principles of selection and order.

It takes our desire to internalize and confirm the ways and power of love.

It takes our willingness to risk, to reach out and to experience shared meaning with our fellow human beings through our gift-giving and grateful receiving.

First and last, it takes being strong enough to love one's whole self and to love others as they are.

The Spiritual Paradox

I have spent over thirty-two years of my life trying to discover and then implement the most profound concept of human self-control, that man is responsible for his own destiny. In my company, we teach rather precisely how, at key moments, we give power away to others that legitimately belongs to ourselves and how we make weakening rather than strengthening decisions. It is common to develop cop-outs that blame others for our problems, or to place our problems into a *time limit* beyond our control, claiming that "I *should* have done something" or "When things get better, I will accomplish a certain task."

The mission statement of my company, "Empowering people to make decisions to control their own lives," is an expression of our work. Our research indicates that about one person in six actually learns what it means to take control of his life and to make life's key commitments, which are these:

• What happens to me is up to me.
• The only time I can control is now.
• I can control my life.

Some individuals, not yet in control of their lives, gradually give in to the notion that they are somehow flawed, weak beyond any strengthening. They develop and actually act out behavior indicating that life is too difficult for them to deal with, too much for them to handle. These mistakes are costly and they rob us of our power. I have written this book to show a road less traveled, another path where we use our power to choose strengthening behaviors and attitudes.

While it may be tempting to become rhapsodic about the loving life, I have attempted to present both ideas and examples to place the flesh of reality on the skeleton of theory. It is not enough to be theoretically right and practically impotent; nor is it enough to blindly follow a "do this" list which is unsupported by understanding. One of the core notions in the Human Valuing System is that *the concept must be married to the skill.*

We have acknowledged that many of the events of life outside oneself are not individually controllable. What is controllable is the way we personally interpret, internalize, and act upon these events. Many far too easily give up on the significant areas of life they *can* control, such as their own state of mind, their ability to find joy and happiness each day, and their capacity to be fully human, regardless of external circumstances.

For those of us who are learning to gain control of our lives and attitudes and to take responsibility for our own happiness, there comes a surprising paradox: *The highest act of self-control is the ability to relinquish that control to a higher power.* At first we resist such an idea; our hard-won freedom and independence feels so sweet. But consider now some larger-than-life facts. For example, none of us are ever "good enough" parents, spouses, or employees; we always fall short of perfection. So far as we can see with our present mind-set, that fact will always be true. So while it is our most important task and legitimate effort to find the ways we can take control of our lives, there will ultimately be times when we cannot exercise control; we all reach the limits of our ability. Then, even when we trust in divine providence, surrender ourselves, and learn all the skills and concepts that lead us to the loving state, we still fall short of the mark. Rather than despair about such an insight, there is another better, far stronger answer.

Learning to Let Go

Differing words with varying degrees of strength help us understand the concept, and hopefully even the practice of letting go. For instance, we know there is a time to simply let go of ideas and philosophies that we have supplanted with better ideas, to let go of principles that we now know are false. There is a time to let go of friendships gone dead, of times and memories no longer magical, of pursuits no longer productive to our growth. A stronger way of expressing this concept is to describe *relinquishment*, which may be defined as that time when I have reached the limits of my capacity to perform, at least in my present state of being or my current problem-solving capacity. I admit that I am incapable of solving all problems, so I relinquish my desire to pretend otherwise.

After years of needing to have all the answers, what a relief it was to me as a high school science teacher to be able to say I did not know the answer and to find that such an admission could be turned into a learning experience for myself and my students. I learned early as a father that I could make honest mistakes in my parenting and that instead of copping out by degrading myself or striking out at my child in anger, I could simply acknowledge I had made a mistake. Then without making either of us the "enemy," we could identify the problem itself and admit that perhaps neither of us knew how to resolve it. Having removed barriers of false pride and pretense, I could then invite my child (who had a mutual interest in making our relationship work) to join with me in working on the problem until we had come to a win/win solution.

We can hold on too long to things which are no longer beneficial, like forever using training wheels on a bike. The key to this letting go process is adopting positive assumptions and stating affirmations positively. Letting go, like all the other crucial changes, begins internally with the adoption of a new value system. We determine to replace tired, judgmental, insecure thoughts with fresh, confident, accepting thoughts.

Crutches We Lay Down

Growing through life's experiences, we learn that there are many common crutches—false beliefs or thought patterns—that we must lay down if we are to walk upright and free. Some of these are listed below.

- Crutch: My value depends on the things I accumulate or on what I accomplish.
- Crutch: My life will be ruined if I lose my loved one.
- Crutch: I need to control my spouse/boss/mother/child/girlfriend.

- Crutch: Every relationship will naturally have a dominant partner and a passive partner.
- Crutch: I am afraid to find out who I really am.
- Crutch: I have to have Bob's/Barbara's support in order to survive.
- Crutch: If only I could change the policy/the deadline/the past/the price, etc.

Affirmations for Daily Living

The most essential affirmation to our well-being and self-esteem is this: "I am valuable just as I am right now." This is, of course, the awareness and acceptance concept of the First Way of Love. The negative version of the same idea would sound something like this: "I must earn my right to be valuable, and others must win my regard. Until worth has been proven, I will view everyone, including myself, suspiciously."

To replace such false thinking that fosters dependent behavior, here are some powerful positive assumptions we may adopt instead:

- I accept all that I cannot change.
- Fear is a creation of my own mind. Without regret or hesitation, I unlock the gate and turn it loose.
- I am a single, pure, harmonious note in the symphony of being.
- Everything affects me and I affect everything.
- The higher power will not diminish me. It is the force which created me, and my creation will be completed as I eagerly immerse myself in its flow again.
- I will go joyfully, eagerly, and fearlessly into the dimensions of mind and being which are beyond thought and the confines of language.
- I know there is pure light at the end of the tunnel. When I align myself with that light, I am in tune not only with myself, but with God.

Letting Go of Dreams and Losses

For many of us, it may seem almost impossible to let go of the dreams we invested in life plans, personal hopes, or in a romance or relationship that didn't work the way we had anticipated. We replay the good times endlessly and ask, "Why wasn't that good enough?" and long for a chance to try again. We replay the bad times and search for the fatal moments. But wallowing in the past only makes things worse. The breakdown of a relationship does not mean that we are bad, or that our life is a failure. More likely it means that we didn't know how to make it work with a particular person, or that the timing for the relationship was poor. The positive assumption that needs to be allowed in such situations is that the *reason* for the failure of the relationship is not what is important; rather, what is important is that we still see ourselves and our efforts as worthy and acceptable.

Another difficult transition for many is the loss of a loved one to death, or the adjustment to a serious disease or injury. One of my dearest friends in life, a vibrant, energetic, charismatic school teacher and mother of three young children, developed cancer in her early thirties. The insidious disease spread and eventually required the removal of much of the skin from her beautiful face. After the operation, she wanted to return to teaching, but feared she and her students could not handle the new reality of her appearance. We spend many hours talking through her feelings as she struggled to accept them. Eventually, she formulated a plan and the determination to try it.

When she finally returned to the classroom, she still harbored great fears of what the students would think and was extremely self-conscious. But on the first day she summoned the courage to stand before her students at the beginning of each class period and say, "I want each of you to look at my face, and I want to look into your eyes so we will not be embarrassed to look at each other." Then she told them the factual story of what had happened. The students were marvelous and totally accepting and many later indicated to me that they were never offended by her appearance.

In spite of her hard-won courage and determination, the cancer eventually took her life. I have been able to accept this fact and to let go only by adopting some positive assumptions, including beliefs founded in my deep and abiding faith that I will someday understand the wisdom or necessity of her death, and that in time, our friendship will bloom again in a realm where there are no diseases and no death.

Surrendering to God

Beyond all this, another concept emerges with even more power than letting go or relinquishment. It might well be called the power to surrender to forces we know we will never control and to powers that now hold (or that we believe now hold) our ultimate destiny. Life itself is such a power. We can learn to feel and express gratitude for having been born—gratitude for the gift of life itself.

In the case of serious illness or debilitating and crippling accidents or other devastating losses, after we have done all we can do, we can then surrender to an infinite power beyond ourselves. The beginning of life is such a time. The ending of life is such a time. The acknowledgement of serious and uncontrollable disease is such a time. Strife, contention, and wars create many countless thousands of such times. That is why some people in their deepest grief or greatest adversities find their deepest meaning and their highest form of self-control in surrendering to the power of God.

One who is not self-controlled, who has not paid the price of learning to take control of his own life, does not have the ability to surrender to God. Because such control has not been learned, the controlling and determining power in life lies in external circumstances, not within the self.

Even after all our good works, we are still incomplete, so surrendering to the grace of God is our most powerful and transcending act. Because we may fear that we will lose our self-control in the process, we may become resistant to being molded and fashioned by the Master Creator. But we must trust in Him who gave us life, believing that He will mold us in a more suitable eternal way. We are at best shortsighted; He is not. We must be able to trust in His omniscience and become willing to give up, or relinquish, our own willfulness. His grace is sufficient to cover our limits.

In effect, each of us, at some significant point in our lives, must either give up in despair, hostility, bitterness, or anger when life-changing events or losses occur, or we must surrender to a higher belief and a higher power, and in that surrender, find our ultimate peace. Serious illness, for example, is often a turning point for becoming bitter or cynical, or it may help us discover deeper meaning, even greater contentment and appreciation for life.

I mentioned earlier in the text that I have suffered serious reversals in my physical health, including at least ten known heart attacks, two quadruple bypass surgeries, a broken back, and more recently, a stroke which partially paralyzed my entire right side. In spite of these challenges and their significant residual effects, I find that I have never felt more genuinely happy, nor have I enjoyed such a degree of acceptance and peace of mind. Music is sweeter and reaches deeper, colors are brighter, smiles and expressions of caring and love are more appreciated, and my prayers are honest talks with God. The comfort I presently need and ask for is the most wondrous and welcomed of comforts. The courage and strength I receive is sufficient for the day.

His grace attends me and I am content in this season of my thanksgiving and peace . . . only because of what I have learned of surrendering to God and living the ways and power of love.

Love lives up to the great truth of God and the universe and puts us in tune with ourselves; it makes us whole.

Given our eternal future, as we seek to become true disciples of Christ and learn how to love our God and our neighbor as ourselves, we can indeed become like our Heavenly Father. We can whisper these great truths to the ends of our being: no force on earth can match the power of love; we have great infinite value; we will live forever as children of God; our heritage is divine. We can rejoice and offer thanksgiving as we come to understand.

Let us carefully consider the ways and power of love. Let us pursue that which matters most: learning to love. Let us recognize the illusions and falsehoods and stop being trapped by them. Freed from those illusions, we can achieve the great commandments of God:

> To love God with all our hearts (thus seeing the world in a new way).
> To love our neighbor (and turn enemies into friends).
> To value and love ourselves, deeply and powerfully.

The ways of love are God's ways. The power of love is God's power. Love is the true pathway to peace . . . our ultimate tie to the divine in ourselves, others, and to God, himself.

THE LOVE/TRUST MODEL

State of Being	Laws Governing Relationships	Motive
Love/Trust	Laws of Love: Spirit of the Law 1. Awareness 2. Selectivity and order 3. Internalization 4. Meaning through gifting-giving 5. Oneness	Motivated by sincere desire and love. Displays "want-to" feelings and behaviors. Makes choices in best, long run self-interest.
Duty/Justice	Laws of Justice 1. The letter of the law 2. The ten commandments	Motivated by duty. Displays "ought-to" feelings and behaviors. "I'll be fair with you if you'll be fair with me."
Fear/Anxiety	Laws of Survival 1. Might makes right 2. Rule of the jungle	Motivated by fear and anxiety. Displays "afraid-not-to" feelings and behaviors. In the active state, thinks, "I'll get you before you get me." In the passive state, does not take responsibility for self and says, "Please take care of me."

| | |
Actions	General Characteristics
1. Goes the extra mile willingly. 2. Believes the world is truly a great place in which to live. 3. Accepts self and others unconditionally.	1. Has good self-esteem. 2. Is trusting and trustworthy. 3. Feels enthusiasm for life. 4. Has self-control. 5. Is serene and happy. 6. Is constantly growing.
1. Thinks, "I'll do my share if you do yours." 2. Believes this adage: "An eye for an eye, a tooth for a tooth." 3. Exerts willpower with a clenched fist.	1. Is consistent. 2. Is a good citizen, worker, and parent on a duty level. 3. Is concerned with what others think. 4. Is technically honest and law-abiding. 5. Is security oriented.
1. Takes care of self first. 2. Feels you can't trust anyone. 3. Does whatever is essential for survival. 5. Employs endless protective covers and shields because of fear.	1. In the active state, is agressive. In the passive state, is withdrawn. 2. Has little or no respect for self or others. 3. Is fearful and suspicious. 4. Needs to control. 5. Seems to have the wrong instincts. 6. Sees the world as an unfriendly place.

Note to the reader:

The ideas and principles contained in *The Ways and Power of Love* were discovered over a period of years. During that time, the concepts were taught in many of C. Kay Allen's classes and seminars. Written information and exercises were provided in those classes to help students use the concepts in their own lives.

The information and exercises used in these classes, along with aphorisms, affirmations, and visualizations that help the reader understand the ideas presented, are available as part of a computer program. To receive information about this program, please write to the following address:

C. Kay Allen
3835 So. Niagra Way
Denver, CO 80237